ISBN: 978-1-879402-17-3
Library of Congress Catalog Number: 2006933087

First U.S. Edition 2006

Published by
Tahrike Tarsile Qur'an, Inc.
Publishers & Distributors of Holy Qur'an
80-08 51st Avenue
Elmhurst, New York 11373-4141
Tel: 718-446-6472 ; Fax: 718-446-4370
www.koranusa.org
read@koranusa.org

Cover Design:
Hubble NGC 4214 Photo - Courtesy of Spaceimages.com

Perspectives on Islamic Faith and History

A Collection of Analytical Essays

Bashir A. Datoo, Ph.D.

Tahrike Tarsile Qur'an, Inc.

Publishers and Distributors of the Holy Qur'an
80-08 51st Avenue
Elmhurst, New York 11373
www.koranusa.org
e-mail: read@koranusa.org

To my beloved parents,
Ahmed and Kulsum,
for providing me with my
grounding in Islam

PREFACE

Islam is a monotheistic religion that is unique in that it is also holistic. It has a system of inter-related beliefs that are organically linked to observance of a set of ritual practices. Together, they guide human beings' relationship not only with their creator, Allah (the Most Glorified and Exalted), but also with His most noble creation, fellow human beings. Thus, Islam regulates the believers' spiritual quest to move ever closer to Allah as well as their secular responsibilities towards others, believers or non-believers alike, and to the environment that they share with other mammals and plants.

The divinely appointed guides, the Prophet, and his successors, the Imams, serve as role models for those who believe in their message and accept their divinity. The Guides, moreover, championed social justice and human dignity centuries before the notions of democratic ideals and human rights became popular. The message of Islam is, thus, truly inspiring but, unfortunately, that message has been lost on the general public.

This collection of essays is intended to bridge the gap between the reality of the Islamic message and its misperception. While each essay stands on its own, collectively they explore the salient aspects of Islamic faith and practice as well as key traits and contributions of the prominent leaders during the formative period of its history.

The essays are more than simply a statement of facts; they seek to go beyond and to provide an explanation of the logic behind those facts. It is hoped that the reader will, thereby, gain a deeper appreciation of Islam and its leading personalities and come to look upon Islam as a magnificent religion and its leaders as principled worthy, respectively, of respect and emulation.

Over the past decade or more, I have authored articles that, as the sub-title of the publication suggests, are intended to give expression to that need of taking religious discourse from the level of description to the next higher level of analysis. Given my own limitations, I'm conscious of the fact that I may not have done justice to this goal, but I sincerely hope that I have made some contribution in that direction.

The majority of the 25 essays assembled in this collection were published in conference proceedings or in local magazines. Since they are all scattered in publications that span a dozen years, they are not readily accessible to many potential readers. I have, therefore, collected them in one publication. I have made minor revisions to the essays to improve upon their content and to make them consistent in their format.

The rest of the essays were prepared specifically for this publication to fill in the gaps in the range of topics that I wished to cover. The intent is to demonstrate that an analytical approach can be applied to any topic, whether it is analysis of beliefs and practices that make up the faith, or analysis of events that occurred in the religion's history.

I hope that readers of these essays will come away with a different, if not a more insightful perspective on Islam. In my attempt to serve Allah's (swt) cause, I humbly seek His forgiveness and mercy for any errors of fact and/or interpretation.

September 2006   Bashir A. Datoo

TABLE OF CONTENTS

4

Note on References and Abbreviations

Unless otherwise stated, the Qur'anic verses cited in this book are from the translation of M. H. Shakir. References to the Qur'an are in the format of (xx:yy) – the number of the sura or chapter is shown before the colon; the number of the ayat or verse is indicated after the colon.

One other source that is cited several times is <u>Nahj al-Balagha [The Peak of Eloquence]: Sermons, Letters and Sayings of Imam Ali b. Talib</u>, compiled by Syed Mohammed Ruzee and translated by Syed Mohammed Askari Jafery.

Many of the other references cited may not be readily available. However, some of these have been digitized and can be accessed at www.al-Islam.org.

The abbreviations shown after the mention of Allah (swt) and the names of the Prophets (s) and Imams (a) are, respectively, a Muslim's way of glorifying God and of sending salutation to the divinely appointed leaders.

TOWARDS THE QUR'ANIC WORLDVIEW
PART I: *TAWHID* (MONOTHEISM)*

Concept of a Worldview

It is essential for any sound worldview, secular or religious, to have certain salient characteristics. It must: offer, as the expression goes, "a 30,000 feet view," a high-level perspective; provide the intellectual foundation for a school of thought; be general at the same time as comprehensive in that it must apply to the totality of the universe and not just to a part of it; be supported by reason and logic, and not be based on emotion or mystique; and be stable from one time period to the next, and eternal, true forever and ever.

However, a religious worldview, including the Qur'anic Worldview, must go beyond the general characteristics enumerated above and have some additional, unique characteristics. It must: give meaning to life, or avow a purpose; give rise to ideals, or lead to aspirations among its adherents; and promote among its adherents commitment to the ideology and responsibility for their actions.**

Essence of the Qur'anic Worldview

"We did not send any Prophet before you except that We revealed to him that there is no other God but Me, so worship me [only]." (21:25)

The essence of the Qur'anic Worldview is captured by the above verse from *Sura al-Anbiya* (The Prophets). The first part of the verse asserts that the message has been uniform and consistent. The message itself is strikingly simple, yet it is profound in its implications. The verse says that there is no God, but Allah (*la illaha illa-Laah*). There is first negation, rejection of all Gods, followed by affirmation, confirmation of One and only One

---

* Published in Towards the Qur'anic Worldview, Report of the Los Angeles 2002 Retreat, published by IEB of NASIMCO, Toronto, 2004
** Characteristics are enumerated in Ayatullah Murtaza Mutahhari, Fundamentals of Islamic Thought: God, Man and the Universe, trans. by R. Campbell, Mizan Press, Berkeley, 1985.

Allah. *Tawhid* is, thus, the all-encompassing reality that constitutes the overarching theme of the Qur'anic Worldview.[*]

The second part of the verse goes on to give a clear, unambiguous command. This command is directed to man, used in the generic sense to include both man and woman, since man is the most noble of creatures (*ashraful makhluq*), endowed with intelligence, the power to think as well as will, the freedom to act. The command follows logically from the unity of Allah (swt), which is to serve Him and Him alone. *Tawhid* has, as its corollary, *Tasleem*. Human beings are, thus, the bridge between the heaven and the earth, the instrument through which the Will of Allah is to be realized on this earth.

Part I of the Qur'anic Worldview

The first part of the essay deals with the overarching theme of *Tawhid* and attempts to break it down into its constituent themes, to decompose it into its component parts. (Please see the diagram at the end of this essay which shows the inter-relationships among the themes/components.) Each component will be introduced with a verse from the Qur'an followed by a brief commentary on the essence and implication of that component.[**]

TAWHID (MONOTHEISM)

"Say: He, Allah, is One. Allah is He on Whom all depend. He begets not, nor is He begotten. And none is like Him." (112:1-4)

The best exemplification of Allah's oneness is *Sura al-Ikhlas* (The Unity) cited above. He is the One and Only God; all other beings are only His creatures. He is Eternal, without a beginning or an end; Absolute, not limited by time or space or subject to any change under any circumstances; the Supreme Reality, the source of all existence; and the Everlasting Refuge, means of comfort in times of distress. Accordingly, we must not think of

---

[*] Muhammad Taqi Misbah Yazdi, At-Tawhid or Monotheism: The Ideological and the Value Systems of Islam, trans. by N. Tawhidi; Sayyid Muhammad Husayni Beheshti, God in the Quran: A Metaphysical Study, trans. by Ali Naqi Baqirshahi, 1996

[**] The commentary draws on S. Mir Ahmed Ali, The Holy Qur'an, 1964, Allamah Sayyid Muhammad Tabatabai, Al-Mizan: An Exegesis of the Qur'an, trans. by Sayyid Akhtar Rizvi (1st 5 chapters), and Fathi Osman, Concepts of the Quran: A Topical Reading, MVI Publications, Los Angeles, 1997.

Him as having a son or a father, for that would reduce the conception of Allah to that of a human being. The only sin that is unpardonable is to associate a partner with Allah (4: 48).

The fact that He is unique in every respect has its logical correlate in the statement that there is nothing that could be compared with Him, thus precluding any possibility of describing or defining Him. Consequently, the quality of His being is beyond the range of human comprehension or even imagination, which is why any attempt at depicting Allah by means of figurative representations, or even abstract symbols is not allowed.

Since Allah's natural reality is beyond human sensory perception, He presents himself in the Qur'an through His attributes or qualities (*asmaul husna* (59:24), "beautiful names"). These qualities help the reader form some impression of Allah and His relation to His creation. Besides, human beings can also be inspired by these qualities as ideals that should guide their morality, while always realizing that they can never achieve Allah's perfection.

CREATION OF THE UNIVERSE

"Allah is He who created the heavens and the earth and what is between them in six periods, and He mounted the throne [of authority] *. . ."* (32:4)

Allah proclaims in the Qur'an that He is the creator of the universe that came into being over a period of time. However, He does not dwell on the act of creation itself for there are only a handful of verses that mention this extraordinary event in a matter-of-fact way. Rather, the Qur'an points to the harmony and coordination in the universe as "signs" of the oneness of Allah.

> *"Most surely, in the creation of the heavens and the earth and the alternation of the night and day, and the ships that run in the sea ..., and the water that Allah sends down from the cloud ..., and the changing of the winds and the clouds made subservient between the heaven and the earth, there are signs for a people who understand."* (2:164)

The Qur'an is not concerned about the processes that led to the creation of the universe, though there are cryptic references to such processes that recent scientific discoveries have begun to fully corroborate (see the essay on The Challenge for the Qur'an, Part II: Temporal Validity). It is enough for Allah to give a command and for the outcome to be exactly what He willed, "*Be, so its is [kun fayakun]*" (36:82). Accordingly, the universe, and all that is within it, reflects His desire for perfection and goodness:

> "... *the handiwork of Allah who had made everything thoroughly* ..." (27:88); "*Who made good everything that He has created* ..." (27:7)

The Intermediate (or Invisible) World

" ... *whoever disbelieves in Allah and His angels and His apostles and the last day, he indeed strays off into a remote error.*" (4:136)

Between the heavens and the earth is the intermediate world that consists of Allah's creation that is "beyond the reach of human sensory perception" (2:3). This creation includes angels who are made out of light and are spiritual beings as well as *jinn* who are made out of fire and are psychic forces. Since they are sharply different from human beings, the two are separated from each other. However, belief in the existence of angels and *jinn* is fundamental in the Islamic faith, though no divinity is to be attributed to them.

Angels are the instruments through which Allah rules the world. Like human beings, they have intelligence but, unlike human beings, they do not have free will. They convey Allah's messages to His prophets, support believers in their actions when He so directs, keep track of human beings' deeds during their lifetime, and gather human souls in death. By contrast, *jinn* have both intelligence and free will. So it is that Allah tests human being and *jinn* by one another. *Jinn* seek to lead human beings astray from the path of righteousness by threats and temptations. Allah warns human being to be wary of *Shaitan* or the Devil:

> " ... *and do not follow the footsteps of the Shaitan; surely he is your open enemy.*" (6:142)

The Earthly (or Visible) World

"And the earth – We have spread it forth and made in it firm mountains and caused [life] *to grow in it of every suitable thing* [in a balanced manner]. *"*(15:19) However, one stands out above all others: *"Certainly We created the human being in the best make."* (95:4)

There is an amazingly great diversity of life on the surface of the earth, below the surface in the soil, above the surface in the sky, and across the surface in the sea. They range from plants and animals, through microorganisms and birds, to fish and other aquatic creatures. These are not, however, haphazard creations that serve merely to demonstrate Allah's enormous creativity. Rather, there is a symbiotic relationship, an intricate interdependence among different life forms such that, when man intervenes in a thoughtless fashion, he disturbs the equilibrium, often with disastrous ecological results.

In addition to the creatures cited above, the earth is also inhabited by human beings who the Qur'an designates as the best of Allah's creation. Unlike the formation of the universe, which, as stated earlier, is described in a perfunctory manner, the creation of man is narrated in exquisite detail in the Qur'an. The various stages of human physical growth are described in a simple way for the ordinary reader, while they can be viewed with great depth by a biologist:

> *"And certainly We created the human being of an extract of clay, then We made him a small seed* [a drop of male sperm {or a female egg}] *in a firm resting-place, then We made the seed a clot* [created out of the male sperm {and the female egg} a mixed suspension), *then We made the clot a lump of flesh* [created out of the mixed suspension an embryo], *then We made* [in] *the lump of flesh bones* [created within the embryo bones], *then We clothed the bones with flesh, then We caused it to grow* [out of all this] *into another creation, so blessed be Allah, the best of the creators."* (23:12-14)

Human beings are unique because they have been given the power of intellect through which they exercise freedom of choice. Accordingly, human behavior is neither dictated only by instinct and biological laws as are those of plants and animals, nor by physical laws as are those of matter. Allah proclaims their special position in the Qur'an thus:

> *"And surely We have honored the children of Adam, and We carry them in the land and the sea, and We have given them of the good things, and We have made them to excel by an appropriate excellence over most of those whom We have created."* (17:70)

PREROGATIVES AND OBLIGATIONS OF THE CREATOR

Allah as the Sovereign

"Surely, Allah upholds the heavens and the earth lest they come to naught; and if they should come to naught, there is none who can uphold them after Him …"(35:41)

As the Creator of the universe, as the mastermind behind its intelligent design, Allah's prerogative is that He is its ruler. Hence, any of the verses that talk of the creation of the universe conclude by stating that He established Himself on the Throne of Authority, knowing and managing all affairs. The declaration of *"All praise is due to Allah, the Lord of the Worlds"* (1: 2) which every Muslim is duty-bound to repeat at least ten times in the daily prayers is to underscore the fact that the Lordship of the being, power, authority and control are wholly in the hands of Allah. However, we need to make a distinction between two different sets of laws that He has put in place:

Natural Versus Divine Laws

" . . . and [He created] *the sun and the moon and the stars, made subservient by His command; surely His is the creation and the command; blessed is Allah, the Lord of the worlds."* (7:54)

" … for every one of you did We appoint a law and a way [of life]*, and if Allah had pleased He would have made you* [all] *a single people, but* [He willed otherwise] *that He might try you in what He gave you, therefore strive with one another to hasten to virtuous deeds … "* (5:48)

The relations, order, balance and coordination that is manifest in various natural phenomena show that these cannot occur haphazardly, but that there is a supreme wisdom and omnipotence that has created and is maintaining the cosmic order in its vastness and complexity. Thus, it is not sufficient to believe that creation is from Allah, but it is also necessary to maintain that their development, interaction, the effects they create and the effects made upon them are all under Allah's management and command.

Human beings have been established on earth as trustees of Allah. One who is entrusted with any power cannot assume absolute right to it, instead, one has to use it according to what the truster, in this case Allah, requires. Thus, we have to acknowledge that the right of law giving belongs only to Allah. His teachings, as embodied in these laws, are designed to direct human behavior to the ideal, to the realization of their full potential. A believer in Allah who is, therefore, aware of all His attributes of full knowledge and wisdom, His care and grace should consistently follow His laws, since true faith in Allah should mean observing what He orders or forbids. Allah's ultimate test for human beings is the extent to which they make the necessary effort to attain the ideal behavior.

Allah as the Sustainer

"And We have made in it [earth] *means of subsistence for you and for him* [all living beings] *for whom you are not the suppliers."* (15:20)

With prerogatives, come obligations. As the Creator of life, Allah has a fundamental responsibility to provide for it. He has, indeed, made provision for all forms of life, with any given level in the hierarchy drawing its sustenance on its next lower level and, in turn, providing sustenance to its next higher level. Being at the apex of the food chain, human beings have, accordingly, been given the responsibility of custodianship of the physical environment. Allah does not make any distinctions among His creatures when it comes to fulfilling His responsibilities. He furnishes sustenance for all, regardless of whether or not they believe in His divinity or accept His message. However, providing for His creatures is not tantamount to spoon feeding them.

General Availability Versus Individual Effort

" ... *and He blessed therein* [the earth] *and made therein its foods, in four periods: alike for the seekers* [equally within reach of all who seek them]. " (41:10)

"And that man shall have nothing but what he strives for." (53:39)

Allah's favors and blessings to human beings are beyond enumeration (14:34). In *Sura al-Rahman* (The Beneficent, 55), Allah cites some of these and, in that relatively short chapter of 78 verses, He punctuates it 31 times with this poignant verse, *"Which, then, of the bounties of your Lord will you deny?"* Allah fully discharges His responsibility by ensuring that provisions are adequate for, and accessible to all the billions of His human beings. He cannot be held responsible for expropriation of those provisions by one group at the expense of another, or for lack of effort on anyone's part to take full advantage of them.

Without that effort, we would not realize that we are creatures in need, beholden to Allah; we would not comply with laws about what is permissible to consume and what is not, and about when we are within our rights and when we encroach on the rights of others. Without that effort, too, science would not make progress in the world and the mysteries of Allah's creation would not be gradually unveiled for all to appreciate His infinite wisdom and generosity.

Breaking down *Tawhid* and *Tasleem* into their Constituent Components

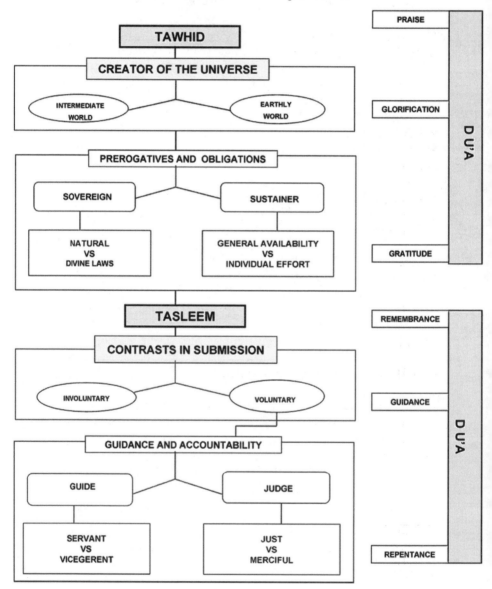

TOWARDS THE QUR'ANIC WORLDVIEW
PART II: *TASLEEM* (SUBMISSION)*

Essence of the Qur'anic Worldview

"We did not send any Prophet before you except that We revealed to him that there is no other God but Me, so worship me [only]." (21:25)

The essence of the Qur'anic Worldview is captured by the above verse from *Sura al-Anbiya* (The Prophets). The first part of the verse asserts that the message has been uniform and consistent. The message itself is strikingly simple, yet it is profound in its implications. The verse says that there is no God, but Allah (*la illaha illa-Laah*). There is first negation, rejection of all Gods, followed by affirmation, confirmation of One and only One Allah. *Tawhid* is, thus, the all-encompassing reality that constitutes the overarching theme of the Qur'anic Worldview.

The second part of the verse goes on to give a clear, unambiguous command. This command is directed to man, used in the generic sense to include both man and woman, since man is the most noble of creatures (*ashraful makhluq*), endowed with intelligence, the power to think as well as will, the freedom to act. The command follows logically from the unity of Allah (swt), which is to serve Him and Him alone. *Tawhid* has, as its corollary, *Tasleem*. Human beings are, thus, the bridge between the heaven and the earth, the instrument through which the Will of Allah is to be realized on this earth.**

Part II of the Qur'anic Worldview

The first part of the essay dealt with the overarching theme of *Tawhid* and the second part deals with its accompaniment, *Tasleem*. (Please see the diagram at the beginning of this essay which shows the inter-relationships among the themes/components.) Each constituent theme of *Tasleem* will be introduced

---

* Published in Towards the Qur'anic Worldview, Report of the Los Angeles 2002 Retreat, published by IEB of NASIMCO, Toronto, 2004
** Ma'alim Muhammedhusein Kermali, An Introduction to Tadabburul Qur'an, IEB NASIMCO

with a verse from the Qur'an followed by a brief commentary on the essence and implication of that theme.*

TASLEEM (SUBMISSION)

"And whatever creature that is in the heavens and that is in the earth makes obeisance [prostration] to Allah [only], and the angels [too] and they do not show pride. They fear their Lord above them, and do what they are commanded." (16:49-50)

Everything existing goes back to Allah as its source and, therefore, is dependent on Him for its beginning as well as for its continued existence. He is, therefore, the Only One who is worthy of being worshipped as is encapsulated in the expression, *"Allah is the greatest" [Allahu Akbar]*, that homage should be paid to none other. Submission to Him is a natural and essential relation between the creation and its creator.

For human beings, submission is not just by tongue alone, by the utterance of *shahadatayn* (profession of faith). This declaration makes a person's body "pure" as he/she becomes a *Muslim* but, in and of itself, it does not lead to the soul's "salvation." It has to be accompanied by innermost conviction, by the attainment of *iman* (right belief) for that person to graduate to the status of a *Mumin*. The Qur'an refers to the dwellers of the desert who claim to "believe (*amanna*)," but Allah instructs His Prophet to correct them by saying that they merely "submit (*aslamna*)" (49:14). For the rest of the universe, submission means compliance with Allah's Will and, hence, it is necessary to contrast its two forms.

CONTRAST IN SUBMISSION

Involuntary Submission

"Do you not see that Allah is He Whom do glorify all those who are in the heavens and the earth ...? He knows the prayer of each one and its glorification, and Allah is cognizant of what they do." (24:41)

---

* The commentary draws on S. Mir Ahmed Ali, The Holy Qur'an, 1964, Allamah Sayyid Muhammad Tabatabai, Al-Mizan: An Exegesis of the Qur'an, trans. by Sayyid Akhtar Rizvi (1st 5 chapters), and Fathi Osman, Concepts of the Quran: A Topical Reading, MVI Publications, Los Angeles, 1997.

Submission is manifested by all His creation, though for all except humankind, it is involuntary through the undisturbed, continuous working of His Will, with perfect harmony. Beyond that, worship of Allah is the sole reason for existence of some entities such as angels, and there is "not a single thing" in the heavens or the earth that does not glorify Allah even if, as the Qur'an tells us, we "do not understand" exactly how (17:44).

Voluntary Submission

"Say: 'O people! Indeed there has come to you the truth from your Lord, therefore whoever goes aright, he goes aright only for the good of his own soul, and whoever goes astray, he goes astray only to the detriment of it, and I am not a custodian over you [responsible for your conduct].*"* (10:108)

The body of a human being, like that of any other living creature, is controlled unwillingly by biological laws, but the mind is capable of voluntarily reaching a belief in Allah and accepting His guidance. The Qur'an pointedly states: *"There is no compulsion in religion"* (2:256). Allah is the Creator and His being is eternal. He fulfills human needs but He is not in need of anyone. Therefore, He is the One to whom human beings have to submit voluntarily if they apply their intelligence properly. Belief should thus come as a conscious decision, not as a result of physical or psychological pressures.

Submission in Islam implies surrender of one's whole being or personality with its thoughts, feelings, aspirations and actions to Allah's guidance. The Qur'an refers to a believer as one who "submits his face (*vajhah*) to Allah" (2:112) since the face is the most expressive part of the body and represents the sum total of a person's personality. The Qur'an warns against any other kind of worship:

"And whoever desires a religion other than Islam, it shall not be accepted from him, and in the hereafter he shall be one of the losers." (3:85)

GUIDANCE FROM, AND ACCOUNTABILITY TO THE CREATOR

Allah as the Guide

"... indeed, there has come to you light and a clear book from Allah. With it Allah guides him who will follow His pleasure into the ways of safety and brings them out of utter darkness into light by His Will and guides them to the right path." (5:15-16)

Allah, however, did not create human beings and leave them to fend for themselves. He intended for their lives to be purposeful so, in addition to general guidance that is granted to all beings, mankind has been blessed with particular guidance that includes inspiration *(ilhaam)* and revelation *(wahy)*. He bestowed upon the Seal of the Prophets, Prophet Muhammad (s), the Qur'an that superseded previous scriptures and that is to prevail until the end of time. The Qur'an laid down the Islamic ideology and the Prophet lived it and so serves as a role model. The message that he brought certainly warned the people about the future, but he had only to convey the message and address the minds and hearts, not to compel or watch over them, since each individual being has intellect and free will and is thus responsible for accepting or rejecting the guidance.

Man's Responsibility: Servant Versus Vicegerent (*Abd* Vs. *Khalifa*)

"O you people! Serve your Lord who created you and those before you so that you may guard [against evil].*"* (2:21)

" ...your Lord said to the angels, I am going to place in the earth a khalifa ..." (2:30)

Human beings' relationship with Allah consists of two dimensions. One may be characterized as the vertical dimension, relationship with the Creator on account of His giving us life and providing us with sustenance. This relationship is one of *abd*, being a passive servant of Allah. As is required of any servant, he/she has to serve his/her master so, too, we have to worship our Lord. *Ibadat* in Islam encompasses every action that is being performed in accordance with Allah's guidance. These actions are not restricted to rituals that are designed to test our willingness to serve Him as He commands, whether they require the sacrifice of time (*salat* or prayers), basic needs (*sawm* or fasting), material comforts (*hajj* or pilgrimage), wealth (*zakat* and *khums* or levy on assets), or even life itself (*jihad* or struggle in the way of Allah).* They extend to include personal character, the development of moral and ethical traits that are meant to reflect the perfection and goodness of Allah. Furthermore, as will be elaborated upon below, *ibadat* has a particular meaning of direct communication with Allah with a view to nurture and strengthen one's consciousness of Allah so that His felt omnipresence inspires us to do good deeds and deters us from bad deeds.

The other dimension of human beings' relationship with Allah may be described as the horizontal one, relationship with His creatures in the spirit of brotherhood among all Muslims and fraternity among all mankind. This relationship is one of a *khalifa*, being active as vicegerent of Allah on the earth. As is incumbent upon any leader, he/she has to cater to his/her followers so, too, we have to be responsive to the needs of individuals and of the society. We have, within the limitations of our capabilities and resources, to work for the establishment of a just and an equitable society by enjoining good (*amr bil maroof*) and forbidding evil (*nahiy anil munkar*). It is this active role that Allah has in mind when He appointed human beings as His vicegerent. For, in the words of the Qur'an, *"Allah does not change the condition of a people until they change it themselves"* (13:11), or, according to a famous English maxim, "God helps those who help themselves."

Allah as the Judge

"What! Did you then think that We had created you in vain and that you shall not be returned to Us?" (23:115)

The Qur'an repeatedly stresses the concept of the individual's full accountability for every deed through the belief in the afterlife. The belief in the individual accountability in the life to come deepens the feeling of personal responsibility in this life.

---

* For an elaboration of these sacrifices, see the essay entitled, "Forms of Worship in Islam."

Allah's Will is to let human beings have the power of thinking and the freedom of choice for only then would it be fair to hold them accountable for what they freely do and what they freely refrain from doing. However, Allah's plan is not to make His judgment and His subsequent requital in this life because He wishes to give human beings a suitable duration for a fair test with the chance of self-correction and improvement. The image of the "clear record" in the verse below portrays how accurate and evident the accountability of each individual will be on the Day of Judgment:

> *"Surely, We give life to the dead, and We write down what* [deeds] *they have sent before and their footprints* [whatever good or evil they have left behind], *and We have recorded everything in clear writing."* (36:12)

Allah's Judgment: Just Versus Merciful (*Adil* Vs. *Rahman*)

"On that Day, all human beings shall come forth in sundry bodies that they may be shown their works [deeds]. *So, he who has done an atom's weight of good shall see it. And who has done an atom's weight of evil shall see it."* (99:6-8)

"Say: O my servants! Who have acted extravagantly against their own souls, do not despair of the mercy of Allah; surely Allah forgives the faults altogether; surely He is the Forgiving, the Merciful." (39:53)

Having furnished human beings with the book of guidance, the Qur'an, and with role models, the Prophet and his immediate progeny, Allah would be perfectly just if, as it were, He goes "by the book," rewards human beings for their good deeds and punishes them for their bad deeds in accordance with what He has clearly laid down. However, Allah is not restricted to judging merely the outcomes since He is All-knowing and is familiar with the intentions behind those outcomes. He will reward a person if he/she had the intention of doing a good deed, even if circumstances prevented him/her from actually carrying it out. But Allah's magnanimity is such that the converse wouldn't apply. Even if a person had an evil intention, Allah will not punish him/her until he/she actually commits a bad deed. When it comes to accounting, though, Allah will never miss an "atom's weight" of good or evil. All will be shown the true worth of everything they did or said in previous life, however hard they may have tried to hide or justify it. The One Allah is All-mighty and His justice will be strict and retribution severe.

At the same time, however, Allah is All-merciful. He has provided human beings with two specific mechanisms to make amends for their bad deeds. One is for a person to recognize the errors he/she made and to seek genuine forgiveness from Allah. Acceptance of forgiveness, however, is conditional upon the person making a concerted effort to change his/her behavior, to avoid the same kinds of mistakes for which he/she has now repented. This has to be done while the person is still alive, while there is still an opportunity to make a good faith effort to reform. Another mechanism comes into play after the person has died and is brought forth to receive Allah's judgment. He/she can plead with the Prophet and the Imams to intercede (seek *shifa*) on their behalf with Allah. Occurrence of intercession, however, is dependent upon whether or not the person had manifested the love of *Ahl al-Bayt* (the Prophet's infallible progeny) in his/her previous life, not through lip service but, rather, through compliance with Allah's commands that pleases the intercessors. The One Allah is All-forgiving when His servants take the necessary, corrective steps to return to the true path whenever they happen to stray away from it.

DU'A

"And when My servants ask you concerning Me, then surely I am very near [to them]; *I answer the prayer of the supplicant when he calls on Me, so they should answer My call and believe in Me that they may walk in the right way."* (2:186)

Given that Allah created and endowed us with all the necessities to live full and productive lives and, given that He guided us to make those lives purposeful and fulfilling, it is incumbent upon us to turn to Him, to supplicate to Him at all times both to recognize His greatness and to seek His favors.

Even though we are not able to see Allah because He is Absolute, He is close to us, closer, in fact, than our "jugular vein" (50:16). When we supplicate to Allah, therefore, He assures us that He can hear us, that He is keenly aware of our innermost wishes. Nay, He even responds but that does not mean that He grants all our desires. Allah knows better what is in our best interests and He may not grant them altogether, or defer them for a period of time to protect us from the adverse after effects that we cannot foresee.

But, most importantly, Allah looks for evidence of reciprocity. If we want Him to fulfill our desires, then He, in turn, expects us to respond to His injunctions. We have to demonstrate complete faith in His wisdom and recognize that the path He has shown us is, indeed, the path that leads to success in this life and in the hereafter. When we step on that path, communion with Allah truly becomes "a two-way street."

Supplication, however, involves more than just asking for one's wishes, be they spiritual or material. As Allah Himself has taught us and as the Imams have demonstrated in the supplications that they have bequeathed to us, it has to include recognition of the Supreme Being to whom these wishes are being directed. Thus, supplication has many different aspects to it. Selected below are those aspects that are directly tied in with various components of the Qur'anic Worldview (see the diagram, again, at the beginning of this essay).

Praise (*Hamd*)

"All praise is due to Allah, the Lord of the Worlds." (1:2)

Supplication begins with the praise of Allah by means of those attributes that are uniquely Allah's, that is, those qualities that refer to His Absolute Perfection. The meaning of absolute perfection is that it is not limited or conditional which makes Allah free of any need.

Glorification (*Tasbih*)

"Glorify the name of your Lord ..." (87:1)

Praise of His qualities is followed by acknowledgement of the outcome of His Will. The beauty and symmetry of the universe and the multitude and diversity of life within it induces us to glorify their Creator.

Gratitude (*Shukr*)

" ... and be thankful to Me, and do not be ungrateful to Me."
(2:152)

Allah is the original source of all good things and blessings. He has bound us by His laws but these laws are, ultimately, for the benefit of mankind. He has provided for our basic needs, even if we have to strive to take advantage of them. On both these counts, human beings have to express, in their supplication, their gratitude for Allah's favors and bounties.

Remembrance (*Dhikr*)

" ... now surely by Allah's remembrance [only] *are the hearts set at rest."* (13:28)

Remembrance of Allah is the basis of *Tasleem*. When true consciousness of the Almighty is inculcated, the human being surrenders completely and utterly to Allah. It is in this unconditional obedience that he/she achieves tranquility since success in this world and in the hereafter is dependent upon it.

Guidance (*Tawfiq*)

"Our Lord! Make not our hearts to deviate after Thou has guided us aright ..." (3:8)

Even after we have submitted voluntarily to Allah's Will, we have to be ever vigilant that we do not stray from the true path. Our supplication has to implore Allah to give us the wisdom and the strength to remain steadfast on that path.

Repentance (*Tawbah*)

"But whoever repents after his iniquity and reforms [himself], *then surely Allah will turn to him* [mercifully] *..."* (5:39)

Human beings have responsibilities to Allah as well as to His creation. But we fall short in our duties so, in our supplication, Allah invites us to repent and, by demonstrating our sincerity in making a behavioral change, ask for His forgiveness.

CONCLUSION

The three areas of *Tawhid*, *Tasleem* and *Du'a* discussed in Parts I and II of the essay are all linked together in a single verse from *Sura al-Fatiha* (The Opening), as is emphasized by the operative words inserted in parenthesis below. It underscores the point that the first area logically leads to the second that, in turn, naturally leads to the third:

> *"Thee* [alone] *[Tawhid] do we serve [Tasleem] and Thee do we beseech for help [Du'a]."* (1:5)

METAPHOR OF CREATION IN THE QUR'AN

Metaphor is a figure of speech in which one object is described as being another object, in other words, two seemingly unrelated objects are being substituted one for the other. That way, the first object is economically described because all the attributes of the second object can be used to fill in the description of the first.

On the one hand, creation of life can be described using the language of natural sciences. It will elucidate the exact process of reproduction. On the other hand, creation can be described using metaphorical language. It will suggest the true purpose behind creation. Allah (swt) employs both types of languages in the Qur'an. He thus satisfies the curiosity of the scientist who seeks to comprehend the marvelous process of creation at the same time as He addresses an inquisitive mind that wishes to understand the deeper meaning of life itself.

Creation in the Scientific Language

When Allah chooses to speak of human beings in a biological sense, that is, a being with a body, He uses the scientific language in *Sura al-Moaminun* (The Believers):

> "*Then we made him a small seed* [*nutfah*, a small quantity of sperm] *in a firm resting place* [*karareen makin*, a reference to genital organs], *then We made the seed a clot* [*alakah*, created out of the male sperm {and the female egg} a mixed suspension], *then We made the clot a lump of flesh* [*muzgah*, created out of the mixed suspension an embryo], *then We made* [in] *the lump of flesh bones* [*ayzamah*, created bones within the embryo], *then We clothed the bones with flesh* [*lahmah*, covered in muscle], *then We caused it to grow* [out of all this] *into another creation, so blessed be Allah, the best of the creators.*" (23:13-14)

The above verses describe, in exquisite detail, the different stages involved in the complex process of reproduction. Dr. Maurice

Bucaille[*] has pointed out that the terms used here, and in other verses scattered throughout the Qur'an, have often been mistranslated due to lack of appreciation of the correspondence between linguistic terms and reproductive processes. Hence, after careful consideration and consultation, he has suggested more appropriate terms that are inserted in parentheses in the verses cited above.

Dr. Bucaille goes on to show how the Qura'n has enumerated the stages of reproduction and how these conform with the scientific knowledge that has been built up only since the nineteenth century. These stages are: performance of fertilization by a very small amount of sperm in association with other constituents of the fertilizing liquid, implantation of the egg in the female genital organs, and evolution of the embryo inside the uterus. Dr. Bucaille concludes: "Everything in the Qur'an is explained in simple terms which are easily understandable to man and [are] in strict accordance with what was to be discovered much later on."

Creation in the Metaphorical Language

When Allah wishes to speak of human beings in a purposive sense, that is, a being with a body and soul, He resorts to the metaphorical language in *Sura al-Hijr* (The Rock) where He talks of the creation of Adam as the symbol of man:

> *"And when your Lord said to the angels: Surely I'm going to create a mortal of the essence of black mud [hamain masnun] fashioned in shape. So when I have made him complete and breathed into him My spirit [ruh], fall down making obeisance to him."* (15:28-29)

The two operative words in the above verses are *hamain masnun* – mud, and *ruh* – spirit. Dr. Ali Shariati[**] has argued that "mud" is the basest material so this metaphor denotes the lowest level to which a human being can sink, whereas "spirit" is the most exalted part of any being so this metaphor connotes the highest

---

[*] The Bible, the Qur'an and Science, trans. by Alastair Pannell, American Trust Publications, Indianapolis, 1979

[**] On the Sociology of Islam, trans. by Hamid Algar, Mizan Press, Berkeley, 1979

level to which a human being can rise. The distance between mud and spirit is the distance between two opposite poles – in one direction lies the lowest of the low, indicative of behavior that is worst than that of animals; in another direction is the highest of the high, suggestive of behavior that is better than that of angels. This distance marks a path, and we call that path religion.

Within us, there are two opposing forces. One is the force of evil, represented by *Iblis* or the Devil, pulling us lower and lower towards mud. Another is the force of good, represented by the *Masumeen* (His infallible guides), pulling us higher and higher towards Allah. There is a constant, fierce struggle – *jihad* – between these two forces. Allah has endowed us with intelligence and has granted us freedom of action. It is, therefore, up to us to choose our direction. Allah has prescribed *ibadat*, acts of worship, which are designed to help induce movement in us in the right direction. Every such obligatory act has to be preceded by *niyya* or intention that includes the key phrase of *qurbatan ilalllah*. The goal is to make us conscious of the purpose of the act that we are about to perform – it is, simply, to bring us closer to Allah. No act can bridge the gap, but every act will shorten the distance.

Conclusion

Allah invites us repeatedly in the Qur'an to ponder over the purpose of life and warns us of accountability for the choice of direction we make in life:

> *"What! Did you then think that We had created you in vain and that you shall not be returned to Us?"* (23:115)

ANALOGY OF LIFE IN THE QUR'AN

Analogy is an analytical tool that is used to describe and/or explain an abstract concept or idea. It involves comparison with a known object or phenomenon. If the comparison is appropriate, then the characteristics of the known object can be transferred to the abstract concept. That way, the concept can be better understood.

The nature of worldly life has fascinated many a literary figure. They have relied on analogy to elucidate it. This essay will, first, examine an analogy that has been used by such literary figures as novelists, playwrights, poets, etc. Next, it will analyze the analogy offered in the Qur'an. This comparison will serve to underscore the beauty and power of Allah's (swt) analogy compared with that of humans.

Literary Figures' Analogy

Among several analogies, that with a candle is the most popular. At first glance, this analogy seems highly appropriate for at least three reasons:

§ Candle has a limited life. It gives light as long as there is a wick to be burned. Life, too, is finite — medical progress can prolong life but, sooner or later, everyone dies.

§ The light of a candle can flicker and go out when there is a gush of wind. The span of life is also unknown — humans can attain or exceed life expectancy, or they can die at any time before that age.

§ The light of a candle is extinguished when the wick is burned but it leaves behind the residue of wax. So, too, when a person dies, the soul departs but the body stays behind.

This analogy of life with a candle is useful because it highlights three salient characteristics of life – that life is finite, uncertain, and ends with the separation of body and soul.

Almighty Allah's Analogy

The analogy in the Qur'an is laid out in *Sura al-Yunus* (Jonah, 10:24) and is supplemented, in one important respect, in *Sura al-Ra'd* (The Thunder, 13:17). Allah compares life to rainwater. At first sight, this analogy seems very odd. However, on reflection, there are at least three fundamental – nay, philosophical – differences between the analogies of a candle and rainwater. The differences can be said to be philosophical because they are tied in with a Muslim's fundamental beliefs and allow him/her to draw practical implications from them.

§ Candle is manufactured by human beings, whereas rain is sent down by Allah. Life, like rain, is a gift of Allah; only He is capable of giving both.

The implication is that we have to do *shukr*, express gratitude to Allah for His favors and bounties, through *dhikr*, remembrance of Allah with a view to surrender completely and utterly to Him.

§ Candle is capable of only giving light, while rainwater gives rise to diverse vegetation of crops, vegetables, fruits, etc. (*"the herbage of the earth of which men and cattle eat grows luxuriantly thereby"*). Human beings, like rainwater, are similarly capable of great and varied achievements. However, they mistakenly come to believe that they deserve the credit (*"when the earth puts on its golden raiment and it becomes garnished ... its people think they have power over it"*). But Allah can demonstrate His power by destroying, in an instant, their achievements (*"Our command* [in the form of natural disaster] *comes to it by day or night so We lay it to waste as though it had not existed yesterday"*).

The implication is that our achievements should not go to our heads and that we should ever be mindful of the fact that we bask in them at the sole pleasure of Allah.

§ Candle stands in place, whereas rainwater flows into watercourses. Life, like rain, continues even after death. Allah goes on to explain that foam, fine bubbles that form at the surface of the water, passes away *("as a worthless thing")* while water itself *("which profits the people")* remains in the earth.

The implication is we leave behind all the material acquisitions when we pass on and take with us only our good deeds from which we will benefit in the hereafter.

The analogy of life with a candle is weaker because the similarities between the two are superficial. By contrast, analogy with rainwater is stronger since it reveals the philosophy behind creation itself.

Conclusion

Following the analogy in *Sura al-Yunus*, Allah, in the very next verse, draws a sharp contrast between this life and the hereafter:

> "[This was an analogy of the worldly life, whereas] *Allah invites* [human beings] *to the abode of peace."* (10:25)

Allah sums up the essence of the worldly life by reminding us not to devote all our energies to this transitory life but to also prepare adequately for the next, eternal life.

THE CHALLENGE FOR THE QUR'AN
PART I: INDIVIDUAL VARIABILITY

Prophets' Need for Miracles

Prophets make a claim that is beyond the experience of ordinary human beings. They declare that Allah (swt) speaks to them directly or through an angel, a truly supernatural event. To prove their claim they, in turn, need a supernatural proof, a miracle of sorts. It should be noted that the miracle is to establish the truthfulness of the messenger, not the veracity of the message itself. Allah, thus, equips all prophets with miracles. The miracles however, have to be appropriate for the society to which the prophets were sent.

During the time of Prophet Musa (Moses), sorcery was widely practiced. One of his miracles, recorded in the Qur'an, is that he turned his staff into a serpent and this serpent next swallowed all the serpents that the magicians assembled to challenge him had fashioned out of their ropes (7:111-118). At the time of Prophet Issa (Jesus), medical sciences were well established. Among his miracles, also recorded in the Qur'an, is that he cured the blind and the lepers, and brought the dead back to life (3:49). All prophets made a point of stressing that they worked miracles *bizni Llah*, by the permission of Allah.

Prophet Muhammad (s), too, showed a few miracles but he did not rely on them to prove his prophethood. The reason is that he was the last of the prophets and his message is for all peoples, and all times. He could not rely on a miracle that could not be seen by future generations. After all, during his time, there was neither camera nor camcorder to record the action for posterity to view. In other words, he needed a lasting, eternal miracle.

Arabs were distinguished for their literary style and were celebrated for their linguistic eloquence. The superiority of a book containing profound knowledge that is beautifully expressed can be testified to by any generation. This is the type of miracle that is fitting for the final prophet. Muslims maintain that the Qur'an revealed to Prophet Muhammad is the verbatim word of Allah. The Meccans demanded the usual kind of miracle: *"Why has not* *a sign been sent down to him from his Lord?"* (6:37), but Allah reminded those who wished to see His sign, that they can see it in the Qur'an: *"We have not neglected anything in the book* [Qur'an]*"* (6:38). Allah's retort was that the Qur'an is, in fact, Prophet Muhammad's greatest miracle.*

Challenge Of Versus For the Qur'an

Skeptics had to be assured of the authenticity of Allah's Book so He declared that even if men and *jinn*, earthly and heavenly beings respectively, were to join forces, they could not bring the "like of Qur'an" (17:88). There are 114 chapters in the Qur'an. Allah first dared them to produce ten similar chapters (11:13) that he then cut back to only one chapter (2:23). There are 6236 verses in the Qur'an. Allah finally defied them to produce "a discourse [*bihadiseen*] like it" (52:34). The intimation was to not only use the Qur'anic language, but also capture the depth of its meaning. This is the challenge *of* the Qur'an, a challenge of inimitability that stands even today.

The Qur'an, in turn, faces its own challenge. It is a guide for mankind: *"Surely this Qur'an guides to that which is most upright ..."* (17:9). It has, therefore, to bring believers back to it over and over again if the guidance is to remain fresh in their minds. The Qur'an is also a guide till the end of time: *"... there is no altering of Allah's creation; that is the right religion ..."* (30:30). It has, thus, to demonstrate its validity over the balance of mankind's history. This is the challenge *for* the Qur'an, a challenge of applicability that has to stand the test of time.

Part I of the Essay

This two-part essay deals with the challenges faced by the Qur'an. The first part tackles the inter-related issues of how the Qur'an contends with the variability in individuals' capacity to comprehend the written word at the same time as it offers the depth of meaning that an individual who reads it repeatedly comes away with an ever deeper appreciation of its message.

---

* Ayatullah Abul al-Qasim al-Khui, The Prolegomena to the Qur'an, trans. by Abdulaziz Sachedina, 2000; Sayyid Mujtaba Lari, The Seal of the Prophets and His Message, trans. Hamid Algar, Islamic Education Center, Potomac, 1989

OUTER AND INNER DIMENSIONS OF THE QUR'AN

The Qur'an meets this challenge by adopting some clever strata-gems. The first stratagem to be discussed here is suggested by the Prophet: "The Qur'an possesses an inner and outer, and the inner contains seven dimensions." Concepts with dual facets have a manifest meaning that requires no further explanation as well as a deeper connotation that demands reflection.

Since Qur'an is a guide, it addresses its teachings to mankind at large so that every man and woman may increase their knowl-edge and perfect their behavior. Thus, at some level, the Book has to be understandable to all. Yet, to communicate subtle ideas that are beyond the realm of material things and sensory experi-ences, verses are imbued with multiple meanings. It is for this reason that two terms are employed to refer to the interpretive processes in Qur'anic studies, namely, *tafsir* and *tawil*. The *tafsir* mode of exegesis is generally used to denote the exoteric or outer meanings of the Qur'an, whereas the *tawil* mode is used to convey its esoteric or hidden meanings. Both modes are es-sential for a fuller understanding of the text of the Qur'an.

Monotheism is the cardinal tenet of Islam. The Qur'an makes this plainly clear: *"And serve Allah and do not associate anything with Him ..."* (4:36). The universe is proclaimed to be unipolar, uniaxial. Its essence is "from Him-ness" (*innah lilah*) and to "Him-ness" (*inna ilayhi rajiun*), that is, our origin is based on His Will, and our return is at His discretion (2:156). The Qur'an, conse-quently, prohibits pre-Islamic Arabs from their worship of idols. On reflection, however, it becomes clear that an idol may exist in any form.

One particularly perilous form is referred to by the Qur'an as *"him who makes his low desire for his god"* (45:23).* To follow one's desire is to worship it, making it another form of idol worship. Thus, one should turn to none other than Allah for help and not to forget Him under any circumstances since, to do otherwise, would direct one's attention away from Him and undermine one's

---

* This illustration is drawn from Allamah Sayyid Muhammad Tabatabai, The Qur'an in Islam: Its Impact and Influence on the Life of Muslims, Zahra Publications, London, 1987.

consciousness of His existential reality. Allah describes such people as "heedless" for *"they have hearts with which they do not understand, and they have eyes with which they do not see, and they have ears with which they do not hear – they are as cattle, nay, they are in worse errors* [more astray]*"* (7:179). For living an ungodly life, their ultimate destination is hell.

HIERARCHY OF ANALYTICAL CONSTRUCTS IN THE QUR'AN

The second stratagem for dealing with individual variability is stated by the Qur'an itself: *"And certainly we have explained for men in the Qur'an every kind of similitude"* (17:89); in another verse, *"And Allah sets forth parables for men that they may be mindful"* (14:25). These comparisons, in fact, involve a variety of analytical constructs all designed to encourage readers to reflect so as to gain enlightenment. The Qur'anic translators lump these constructs together as parables because they fail to make the subtle distinctions among them. The constructs can, in fact, be arrayed in a hierarchy, from relatively simple constructs that most readers can readily understand to ones that are comparatively complex that only a minority with analytical capabilities can appreciate. Discussed below is one example of each of four constructs; the examples have been selected to illustrate some of the most fundamental beliefs and values of Islam.

Parable

The simplest of the constructs is a parable. It is a simple story that engages the reader. But there is a definite purpose to it, namely, to illustrates a moral lesson. A reader who grasps the lesson is expected to apply it in his/her daily life.

> *" ... When he* [Prophet Ibrahim (Abraham)] *said to his father and his people: What are these images to whose worship you cleave? They said: We found our forefathers worshipping them. He said: Certainly, you have been* [both] *you and your fathers, in manifest error. They said: Have you brought to us the truth, or are you one of the triflers? He said: Nay! Your Lord is the Lord of the heavens and the earth, Who brought them into existence, and I am of those who bear witness to this."* (21: 52-56)

"And by Allah! I [Prophet Ibrahim (Abraham)] *will
certainly do something against your idols after you go
away, turning back. So he broke them into pieces, except the chief of them, that haply they may return to it.
... They said: Have you done this to our gods, O
Ibrahim? He said: Surely* [some doer] *has done it; the
chief of them is this, therefore ask them, if they can
speak. ... They were then made to hang down their
heads: Certainly you know that they do not speak. He
said: What! Do you then serve besides Allah what brings
you not any benefit at all, nor does it harm you?"* (21:
57-58, 62-63, 65-66)

This story of Prophet Ibrahim (Abraham) begins with a ruler,
named Namrud, who reigned over Babylon. When he became
very powerful, he called on his subjects to worship him as their
lord. Since they themselves had fallen into polytheism and were
worshipping idols carved out of wood and stone, they readily
accepted him as their god. Allah then sent them a messenger,
Prophet Ibrahim, so as to guide them to the right path. He reasoned with them that the idols are not worthy of being worshipped. Worship is reserved only for the One and the only One
Allah who is the Creator and the Lord of the heavens and the
earth. His arguments fell on deaf ears.

The people used to celebrate a festival every year outside the
town. When everyone had left town, Prophet Ibrahim demol-
ished all idols with a pickaxe except the biggest one. He spared
it because he wanted to use it in defense of his action and to
teach the people a lesson. When they returned, they were very
upset and suspected Prophet Ibrahim of being the culprit. He
maintained that it must have been done by the bigger idol and,
if he is in a position to speak, he can verify it. They could not
but acknowledge helplessness of their lords. Prophet Ibrahim
seized this opportunity to demolish the very cult of idolatry
when he told them that they worship pieces of wood and stone
that do not benefit or harm them. Eventually, Namrud summoned him to inquire about the Lord to whom he was inviting
his subjects to worship. Fearful of the cogency of his arguments,
the ruler ordered him exiled from his kingdom so that nobody
could embrace his religion.

Analogy

Next in the hierarchy of constructs is an analogy. It involves comparison with a known object or phenomenon. If the comparison is appropriate, then the characteristics of the known object can be transferred to the abstract concept. That way, the concept can be better understood. One profound analogy, that of life itself, is discussed in a separate essay entitled, "Analogy of Life in the Qur'an." Here, another analogy, that of alms giving, will be described.

> " ... *do not make your charity worthless by reproach and injury, like him who spends his property* [wealth] *to be seen of men ...; so his parable is as the parable of a smooth rock with earth upon it, then a heavy rain falls upon it, so it leaves it bare; they shall not be able to gain anything of what they have earned ...* " (2:264)

> " *And the parable of those who spend their property* [wealth] *to seek the pleasure of Allah and for the certainty of their souls is as the parable of a garden on an elevated ground [hillside], upon which heavy rain falls so it brings forth its fruit twofold but if heavy rain does not fall upon it, then light rain [is sufficient]; and Allah sees what you do.* " (2:265)

Charity is highly stressed in Islam. It takes different forms, some of which are obligatory and others of which are optional. However, when this act of charity is carried out simply to show off to others, or is followed by reproach to the recipient, it becomes null and void. The analogy that Allah uses is that of a smooth rock covered with little soil. Now, the two most important ingredients for plant growth are soil and rain. But, in a heavy downpour, the soil is washed away and the bare rock is exposed. It cannot absorb water so it cannot nourish a seed to grow. Similarly, a person who does a good deed, but not with the intention of seeking Allah's pleasure, is like that smooth rock. It is incapable of receiving divine mercy and grace.

By contrast, a person who avoids those twin pitfalls – that is, does not seek to impress others and does not follow it up with a reprove — is like the analogy of a garden on a hillside. When the rain falls, the soil is well drained so plant life flourishes and brings forth abundant fruits. The yield may vary in quality and quantity depending upon the amount of rain. Precisely because of this variation, the verse ends with the assurance of Allah's perfect knowledge of a benefactor's intentions and, therefore, of His proportionate reward for the good deed.

Metaphor

Third in the hierarchy of constructs is a metaphor. It is a figure of speech in which one object is described as being another object, in other words, two seemingly unrelated objects are being substituted one for the other. That way, the first object is economically described because all the attributes of the second object can be used to fill in the description of the first.* A metaphor is higher up the hierarchy than is an analogy because the latter is aspectual, whereas the former is holistic. One vivid metaphor, that of creation, is discussed in another essay entitled, "Metaphor of Creation in the Qur'an." Below is described another metaphor, that of religious beliefs and practices.

> *"Have you not considered how Allah sets forth a parable of good word [kalemah] [being] like a good tree, whose root is firm and whose branches are in heaven, yielding its fruit in every season by the permission of its Lord?"* (14:24-25)

> *"And the parable of an evil word [kalemah] is as an evil tree pulled up from the earth's surface; it has no stability."* (14:26)

The word "*kalemah*" used in these verses is, in its widest sense, word spoken by Allah and so is usually interpreted as the Divine Message, the True Religion. Islam consists of a two-part system that are inter-related and cohesive. Beliefs are like the metaphor of roots of a tree which, if they are firm in the believers' hearts, will affect their actions. These actions constitute the metaphor of branches of the tree and, as the roots strengthen, the branches grow and eventually flowers blossom and bear fruits. There is, moreover, interaction between the two so, just

---

* The only difference between a metaphor and a simile is that a simile makes the comparison explicit by using "like" or "as."

as initially the roots cause the development of branches so, too, later on the branches, through a feedback mechanism, help the roots to penetrate the ground more deeply. Thus, the stronger the faith the more sincere is the practices and, the greater the compliance with practices, the more secure is the faith. The tree, then, does not just yield fruits in a particular season, rather, it bears them all year round. This fruit is nothing other than felicity both in this life and in the hereafter.

On the other hand, weak faith is like the metaphor of a tree whose roots are relatively shallow and, consequently, it is not very stable. Such a tree will not only bear no fruit but, before long, will start to decay and eventually die. This Qur'anic metaphor has inspired Islamic scholars to refer to beliefs as *Usul ad-Din*, the Roots of the Religion, and religious practices as *Furuh ad-Din*, the Branches of the Religion. It has been related by Imam Musa al-Riza, the Eight Imam in the line of succession to the Prophet, that: "A tree is not complete without its roots sunk deep, its trunk firm and its branches starting high. Likewise Islam or the faith is proved by Three Things: Conviction at heart, Declaration in words and Practice strictly as prescribed."

Allegory

The most advanced of the constructs is an allegory. This is an extended metaphor in which objects or persons in a story are equated with the meanings that lie outside of the story itself. The underlying meaning has, in the context of the Qur'an, a religious significance and characters are often personification of abstract ideas.

> *"Surely Qarun* [Korah] *was of the people of Musa* [Moses] *... and We had given him of the treasures, so much so that his hoards of wealth would certainly weigh down a company of men possessed of great strength. When his people said to him: Do not exult, surely Allah does not love the exultant. And seek by means of what Allah has given you the future abode, and do not neglect your portion of this world, and do good* [to others] *as Allah has done good to you and do not seek to make mischief in the land ..."* (28:76-77)

"He said: I have been given this only on account of the knowledge I have. Did he not know that Allah had destroyed before him of the generations those who were mightier in strength than he and greater in assemblage? ... (28:78)*

Qarun (Korah) was a cousin of Prophet Musa (Moses). He was one of those who believed in the ministry of Prophet Musa but, when Allah tested him with the abundance of wealth, he chose the way of tyranny, oppression, coercion and arrogance. Both men were, at the time, traveling in the desert so Qarun's treasures were presumably left behind in Egypt and only the keys were carried. The treasures must have been so immense that the keys of the chests in which they were stored proved heavy even for a band of stalwarts. Qarun was advised not to exult in his wealth for three evils may follow: its possessor may be a miser, he may be oblivious of the needs of the less fortunate, and he may use it to further corruption. He, apparently, had all these three vices.

Qarun maintained that it wasn't Allah who had blessed him with all his wealth. Rather, he had earned it himself on account of his knowledge or acumen. The Qur'an relies on an allegory to portray him as the personification of arrogance and avarice, of evil incarnate. Allah warns that He had destroyed the likes of Qarun in previous generations in this world itself. Indeed, Qarun suffered the same fate when the earth swallowed him and, to drive home the point, the Qur'an stresses that *"he had no body of helpers to assist him against Allah"* (28:81).

Conclusion

Imam Ali b. Talib (a), the First Imam in the line of succession to the Prophet, has provided the most beautiful description of the salient characteristics of the Qur'an in *Nahj al-Balagha*. Extracted below are its characterizations that are particularly germane to the theme explored in the first part of this essay:

> "Then God revealed to him [the Prophet] the Book. It is... an ocean whose depth shall not be fathomed ... it is the fountainhead of knowledge in its vastness ...an ocean that shall not be drained by those who draw upon it; a spring that shall not be exhausted by those who draw from it; a watering place that shall not be depleted by

those who come to it ... the hilltops that cannot be bypassed by those who seek them ..."

THE CHALLENGE FOR THE QUR'AN
PART II: TEMPORAL VALIDITY

Challenge Of Versus For the Qur'an

Skeptics had to be assured of the authenticity of Allah's Book so He declared that even if men and *jinn*, earthly and heavenly beings respectively, were to join forces, they could not bring the "like of Qur'an" (17:88). There are 114 chapters in the Qur'an. Allah first dared them to produce ten similar chapters (11:13) that he then cut back to only one chapter (2:23). There are 6236 verses in the Qur'an. Allah finally defied them to produce "a discourse [*bihadiseen*] like it" (52:34). The intimation was to not only use the Qur'anic language, but also capture the depth of its meaning. This is the challenge *of* the Qur'an, a challenge of inimitability that stands even today.

The Qur'an, in turn, faces its own challenge. It is a guide for mankind: *"Surely this Qur'an guides to that which is most upright ..."* (17:9). It has, therefore, to bring believers back to it over and over again if the guidance is to remain fresh in their minds. The Qur'an is also a guide till the end of time: *"... there is no altering of Allah's creation; that is the right religion ..."* (30:30). It has, thus, to demonstrate its validity over the balance of mankind's history. This is the challenge *for* the Qur'an, a challenge of applicability that has to stand the test of time.

Part II of the Essay

This two-part essay deals with the challenges faced by the Qur'an. The second part tackles the issue of how the Qur'an demonstrates that its message will be valid until the end of time. The evidence is sprinkled throughout the Qur'an and relates to every period in human history, beginning with the Prophet's own lifetime and ending when this world, according to Islam, will come to an end. Illustrative examples discussed below include one that occurred in the short-term, during the time of the Prophet; two that happened in the medium-term during the following twelve centuries; and one that occurred or is yet to occur, in the twentieth century or beyond respectively.[*]

---

[*] Some of the examples of truths are drawn from Maurice Bucaille, The Bible, the Qur'an and Science, trans. by Alastair Pannell, American Trust Publications, Indianapolis, 1976, and of prophecies from Ayatullah Abul al-Qasim al-Khui, The Prolegomena to the Qur'an, trans. by Abdulaziz Sachedina, 2000.

SCIENTIFIC TRUTHS ALLUDED TO IN THE QUR'AN

The Qur'an uses two basic approaches to establish its claim of finality. The first is mentioned in the Qur'an itself: *"And certainly We have brought them a Book which We have made clear with knowledge ..."* (7:59). This approach relies on explanation, making plain the mysteries of natural phenomena. The explanations, however, are terse because Qur'an is a book of guidance, not a treatise on science. Importantly, they are not presented as theories that might be subject to change, rather, they are stated as truths that would later be confirmed with the advancement of science. The trick, though, was to express these scientific truths in a way that would make some sense to the *ummah* or community of the Prophet at the same time as they would be pointers for later day scientists.*

Truth Discovered in the Short-Term

"Therefore, [for] *whomsoever Allah intends that He would guide him aright, He expands his breast for Islam, and* [for] *whomsoever He intends that He should cause him to err, He makes his breast strait and narrow as though he were ascending upwards ..."* (6:125)

The Qur'an describes the feeling of discomfort that one experiences at high altitude as air thins and oxygen decreases. This is, of course, why mountaineers have to carry a supply of oxygen and cabins of airplanes have to be pressurized. The Arabs of the desert of the Arabian Peninsula may not have known about this phenomenon. However, in the southwest corner of the Peninsula is Sana in the Yemen, a town that is at a height of 7900 feet above sea and was inhabited in the seventh century. So, as Islam spread within the Peninsula itself during the lifetime of the Prophet, this knowledge must have become common.

Truths Discovered in the Medium-Term

"Glory be to Him Who created pairs of all things, of what the earth grows, and of their kind and of what they do not know." (36:36)

---

* Since the Qur'an was translated by scholars with linguistic skills, they didn't always select appropriate words to convey what turned out to be scientific ideas. Thus, the treasure trove of scientific truths contained in the Qur'an didn't become evident for a long time.

While it was obvious that a man and a woman have to come together for reproduction to occur, even if the process itself was not understood, it was not until the eighteenth century that researchers became aware of fertilization in plants and learned that every living being comes into existence as the result of merging of a male and a female cell. Generally, fertilization among plants takes place through microscopic particles under the agency of insects, bees, etc., together with the most potent of them all, wind. It is interesting that, after setting forth this principle of two genders, the Qur'an enlarges the scope to embrace all parts of existence that "they do not know" (compare also *"And of everything we have created pairs that you may be mindful,"* 51:49). Only recently has man come to realize that all substances in the world can be reduced, in the final analysis, to their smallest structural unit, the atom. This infinitely small unit itself comprises a duality, one of which carries a positive electrical charge and the other a negative one. When attraction between the opposite poles is exerted, a third entity comes into being – a force that is neutral in its electrical charge.

"Then He turned to the heaven and it was smoke [dukhan], and He said to it and to the earth: 'Come! Willingly or unwillingly!' They said: 'We come heartily.' Then He set them up as seven heavens in two days [periods] *...We have adorned the lowest heaven with lamps* [stars] *..."* (41:11-12).

"Have the faithless not regarded that the heavens and the earth were interwoven [ratq used to refer to the process of fusing, binding together*], and We disjoined them [fatq,* used to refer to the action of breaking, separating out*] ..."* (21:30).

"We have built the sky with might, and indeed it is We who are its expanders." (51:47)

(The translation of these verses is by Ali Quli Qara'i[*])

The Qur'an succinctly describes the origin of the universe in these few verses. Modern day scientific thinking is that the solar system was once a big smoke or gaseous mass *("dukhan"* in the

---

[*] The Qur'an with a Phrase-by-Phrase English Translation, ICAS Press, London, 2004

Qura'nic word) that was slowly rotating. This nebula, through a process of condensation and contraction, subsequently split up into huge, multiple fragments that were to give birth to the galaxies. The fragments further split up into stars and, as a result of a complex series of forces and processes, left the Sun and planets in their places, among them the Earth. Finally, as has been recently established, the distant galaxies are moving away from the solar system and from each other. The universe, therefore, is not in a state of immobility and balance as was previously thought, rather, it has been described as "a soap bubble or a bellows in its constant expansion." Its origin, as revealed by the Qur'an, shows some, if not all likeness to the scientific thinking as it has so far evolved. It should be stressed that while the scientists are interested in "how," that is, the processes that led to the creation of the universe, the Qur'an focuses on "who," that is, the agency that brought about those processes. For the Qur'an wants human beings to reflect on the magnificence of creation in order to cultivate in them the consciousness of Allah.

Truth to be Discovered in the Long-term

"And one of His signs is the creation of the heavens and the earth and what He has spread forth in both of them of living beings [dabbatin]; and when [iza] He pleases He is all-powerful to gather them together." (42:29)

The word *dabbatin* in this verse is used for living creatures of all kinds as evidenced by its definition in another verse *("And Allah has created from water every living creature [dabbatin]: so of them is that which walks upon its belly, and of them is that which walks upon two feet, and of them is that which walks upon four; Allah creates what He pleases ..."* (24:45)). The Qur'an, thus, unequivocally indicates the existence of biological life on other planets. As far as our solar system is concerned, scientists don't entertain the possibility of finding conditions similar to those on Earth on another planet in this system. However, their existence outside of it is considered quite probable because the stars, like the sun, rotate very slowly, a characteristic that suggests that they are surrounded by planets that are their satellites. The Qur'an underscores the plurality of the worlds by its reference to Allah as the *"Lord of the Worlds"* (*aalameen*, 1:2). Exploration of space has yet to conclusively confirm the presence of life outside of the planet earth but, because *iza* in the verse above means when, not if, mankind can expect Allah to someday "gather them together."

DEFINITIVE PROPHECIES MADE IN THE QUR'AN

The second approach for establishing the Qur'an's finality is indicated by Ali b. Abi Talib (a): " The Qur'an contains the knowledge of the past and that of the future up to the Day of Resurrection ..." Knowledge of the past could be verified by comparison with scriptures of other monotheistic religions and/ or by events that were recorded in history. Knowledge of the future involves prediction, foretelling significant events that have yet to occur. These predictions, moreover, are not based on any probabilistic assessment that carries the risk of not being realized, rather, they are based on divine knowledge that has the certainty of being fulfilled in due course.

Prophecy Fulfilled in the Short-Term

"The Romans are vanquished, in a near land, and they, after being vanquished, shall overcome, within a few years. Allah's is the command before and after; and on that day the believers shall rejoice... [This is] Allah's promise! Allah will not fail His promise, but most people do not know." (30: 2-4, 6)

At the time of the Prophet, there were two superpowers: the Roman Empire in the West and the Persian Empire in the East. Each sought to achieve dominance so there were constant wars between them. In 614-15 A.D., the Persian Empire managed to defeat the Roman Empire and the Romans lost control of Jerusalem and other important cities. The Meccan idolaters rejoiced at the news of the defeat of the God-worshipping Byzantines by the fire-worshipping Persians because they saw, in the sack of Jerusalem, a good omen for their own struggle against the Muslims. Within a few years, however, the Romans won an important battle in 622 A. D. and successfully penetrated Persia in the next two years. By that time, the Prophet had already migrated from Mecca to Medina, two towns in the Arabian Peninsula, and in the same year (624 A.D.) that the Romans completed their conquest of Persia, the Muslims vanquished the

Meccans in the first defensive battle against them, at the Battle of Badr. The Qur'an's prophecy, made in no uncertain terms, was fulfilled to the letter.

Prophecies Fulfilled in the Medium-Term

"He it is Who raised among the inhabitants of Mecca an Apostle from among themselves, who recites to them His communications and purifies them, and teaches them the Book and the Wisdom, although they were before certainly in clear error. And others [aakhareen] from among them who have not yet joined them ... That is Allah's grace; He grants it to whom He pleases ..." (62:2-4)

These verses were revealed in Medina when Muslims still comprised a small community. Furthermore, they were at that time struggling against heavy odds with the Meccan adversaries and their confederates and no one could imagine that Islam would spread beyond the city-state of Medina, let alone the boundaries of the Arabian Peninsula. The Prophet was sent as a blessing to the whole universe with the inherent promise that Islam will be the reality for all the peoples of the world. While Muslims conquered parts of the Roman and Byzantine Empires within a decade of the Prophet's demise, the majority of the people of *aakhareen* (that is, non-Arabs), consisting of different races and cultures and living outside of the main centers, did not come into the fold of Islam until a full century later.

" O assembly of the jinn and the men! If you are able to pass through [penetrate] *the regions of the heavens and the earth, then pass through* [penetrate]*; you cannot pass through* [penetrate] *but with authority* [a power]. (55:33)

The translation of this passage requires an explanation before its import can be appreciated; the explanations are from Dr. Maurice Bucaille's book. The word "if" in English is a condition dependent upon a possibility that is achievable or unachievable. But, in Arabic, three different words are used to capture these three states of possibility, achievability and non-achievability. The verse in question uses *in* which represents an achievable possibility so Qur'an talks about the possibility of a concrete realization. The word "penetrate" is the translation of the verb *nafada* followed by the proposition *min* which means to pass through and come out on the other side of a body. The

Qur'an thus suggests a deep penetration and emergence at the other end. Finally, the word "power" indicates that this feat cannot be achieved but with the aid of some mechanical power. This verse, therefore, clearly intimates the possibility that man will one day conquer space, a feat that was, indeed, spectacularly achieved first by the Russians when they launched their sputnik into space in 1960.

Prophecy to be Fulfilled in the Long-Term

"He it is Who sent His Apostle with guidance and the religion of truth, that He might cause it to prevail [liyuzheerah] over all religions, though the polytheists may be averse." (9:33; repeated in 48:28 and 61:9)

"Allah as promised to those of you who believe and do good that He will most certainly make them rulers [layastakhlifannahum, alternatively translated as inheritors or successors] *in the earth as He made rulers those before them, and that He will most certainly establish for them their religion which He has chosen for them, and that He will most certainly, after their fear, give them security in exchange ..."* (24:55; repeated in 21:105 and 28:5)

The two verses cited above are inter-related in that the first prophesizes an event and the second an outcome that is contingent upon that event. Both verses, in turn, depend on the agency that would bring about the event. Muslims believe that the agency is the person of Imam al-Mahdi (a) (The Guided), the Twelfth and the Last of the Imams in the line of succession to the Prophet, who will emerge from occultation towards the end of time. It is he who will see to it that Islam "prevails" over all other regions, be they monotheistic or polytheistic. And, when Islam reins supreme, and the earth is filled with justice and equity after being filled with injustice and inequity, the faithful and the righteous will be its "inheritors." Such is the certainty of the prophecies that, as indicated above, Allah repeats each three times in the Qur'an. There is, indeed, external corroboration of the prophecies from the innumerable traditions, traced back to the Prophet and the Imams, which describe the multitude of "signs" that will precede the reappearance of al-Mahdi. When these traditions were recorded, nobody could have foretold how events, attitudes, lifestyles, morals, etc. would change over time. Yet, we have seen in our century, that many of these signs ring true so it is only a matter of time before al-Mahdi reappears.

Conclusion

Imam Ali b. Talib (a), the First Imam in the line of succession to the Prophet, has provided the most beautiful description of the salient characteristics of the Qur'an in *Nahj al-Balagha*. Extracted below are its characterizations that are particularly germane to the theme explored in the second part of this essay:

> "Then God revealed to him [the Prophet] the Book. It is a light whose radiance shall not be extinguished; a lamp whose flame shall not die ... a blaze whose brilliance shall not be darkened ... an elucidation whose cornerstones shall not be demolished ... the valleys of the truth and its fields ..."

"BOOKEND" REVOLUTIONS IN ISLAMIC HISTORY*

Revolutions usher in a sudden change. A well-planned and successfully launched revolution brings about transformation of the society through an overhaul of its institutions. "Bookend" revolutions mark the two ends of a major historic era. The era that is the focus of this essay is the period that began with the proclamation of the Islamic message by Prophet Muhammad (s) and that will end with the revival of that same message by the Twelfth and the last representative in the line of succession to the Prophet, Imam al-Mahdi (a).

The First Revolution

The Prophet was born in Mecca in 570 A.D. into a society that was torn by fratricidal wars and inter-tribal feuds, sunk in ignorance, addicted to obscene rites and superstitions, and marked by lawlessness and cruelty. He had to live through it for forty long years. Yet he needed the time to impress upon the Meccans two salient personal traits that would enable him to initiate his revolution, namely, truthfulness and trustworthiness. The Meccans had to believe that the Prophet told nothing but the truth (he was *sadik*) and that he could be trusted (he was *ameen*) under any circumstances.

The Prophet had come not to fit into a mold, but to break the mold. He thus introduced a comprehensive code of life, a code that made no artificial distinctions. At a societal level, it did not separate "church" from "state," distinguish conduct of personal, spiritual behavior from regulation of administrative, secular affairs. At a personal level, it did not promote *ibadat* at the expense of *muamalat*, religious observances to the neglect of social responsibilities. The religion of Islam offered mankind a truly holistic worldview.

There was no "lonelier" person than the Prophet at the beginning of his mission in 610 A.D. He had gained few converts and faced virulent opposition. This opposition began with ridicule and harassment and rapidly accelerated into an economic boycott and a threat to his personal life. It was not until he migrated

---

* Published in <u>Az-Zahra</u>, Volume 4, Issue 3, New York, November 2003

to Medina in 622 A.D., another town in Saudi Arabia, and established a city-state there that Islam began to take hold. During his own lifetime, Islam had spread to most of the populated areas of the Arabian Peninsula and some converts were to be found as far afield as Syria and Iraq.

Buoyed by the quickening pace of his revolution, the Prophet wrote letters and sent emissaries to neighboring rulers and heads of other religions to invite them to the fold of Islam. He set the stage for what unfolded, diffusion of Islam through vast areas of the Old World in the succeeding centuries. This was not achieved, as historians had previously alleged, by the force of the "sword," rather, as they themselves now readily acknowledge, by the intrinsic "appeal" of the message itself. This appeal had to do with the emphasis that Islam laid on the moral and ethical development of the individual and the establishment of a just and equitable society. [*]

The Final Revolution

Since the demise of the Prophet in 632 A.D., even as Islam spread widely, the Muslim *ummah* or community began to deviate from the principles and the values that he had taught. Notwithstanding short periods in history when there were attempts to reform the *ummah*, the deviations have, in fact, multiplied manifold. The extent is abundantly clear from the "signs" that have been foretold in the traditions that herald the reappearance from occultation of Imam al-Mahdi.

There will be no "stranger" religion than Islam at the end of time. The religion will have undergone so drastic a change that it will not even be recognized as the religion of Islam. When Imam al-Mahdi reappears, it will not be to introduce a new religion but, rather, to reintroduce the same religion. His task will be to purge Islam of all its distortions and innovations, to distill it to its original essence. Whereas the Prophet's mission was to present Islam to mankind, al-Mahdi's charter will be to purify it for humanity.

---

[*] Conditions in pre-Islamic Arabia and the hardships faced by the Prophet are described in Jafar Subhani, The Message, 1984, and Sayed Ali Asgher Razwy, A Restatement of the History of Islam and Muslims, published by the World Federation, London, 1997.

Just as the Prophet initially had few converts among the hordes of Meccan pagans so, too, Imam al-Mahdi will at first have limited supporters, 313 according to one tradition, among the mass of Muslims. The means by which he will succeed to universally communicate his message and bring about wholesale conversions has, hitherto, been something of an enigma. However, with the advent of the information revolution and innovations in military technology, it is now becoming possible to imagine his path to success.

Muslims have no doubt about the eventual success of al-Mahdi's revolution. For, as Allah (swt) has promised in the Qur'an, Islam will eventually "prevail" (*liyuzheerah*) over all other religions (9:33). Prevail is not used in the narrow sense to indicate that it will be ascendant over Abrahamic religions for, Muhammad as the Seal of the Prophets, had already accomplished that feat. Rather, prevail is used in the broad sense to imply that it will be triumphant over all other religions, including polytheistic religions. Islam will, once again, rein supreme.[*]

Agency of Change

Revolutions do not just occur by chance. A study of history and a reading of the Qur'an suggest that there are fundamentally two forces that bring it about, that there are two agencies of socio-political change.[**] Which of the two agencies is pre-eminent at what point in history is, generally, a function of the level of the development of a society and, in the Islamic context, of the stage of evolution in its submission to Allah.

At the time of the birth of the Prophet, the Meccan society was at a primitive level of human development. Hence, the force of personality, the vision of a leader was the dominant mechanism in launching a revolution. The importance of the twin qualities of the Prophet's truthfulness and trustworthiness now become clear. The Qur'an hints at the role of the Prophet as a revolutionary:

---

[*] Questions concerning the occultation and reappearance of the Imam are explored in Ayatullah Ibrahim Amini, Al-Imam Al-Mahdi: The Just Leader of Humanity, trans. by Abdulaziz Sachedina, Islamic Education & Information Center, Toronto, 1996, and Ayatullah Lutfullah Safi Gulpaygani, Discussions Concerning Al-Mahdi, trans. by Sayyid Sulayman Ali Hasan, Islamic Humanitarian Service, Kitchener, Canada, 2000.
[**] These ideas are advanced by Ali Shariati, On the Sociology of Islam, trans. by Hamid Algar, Mizan Press, Berkeley, 1979.

"Even as We sent among you an Apostle from among you who recites to you Our signs and purifies you and teaches you the Book and the wisdom and teaches you that which you did not know." (2:151)

At the time of the reappearance of Imam al-Mahdi, the global society will have reached an advanced stage of human development. Consequently, the force of *"al-nas,"* the will of the people will be the primary mechanism in bringing about the revolution, albeit, under the leadership of the Imam. The Qur'an has intimated the role expected of the followers:

"Surely, Allah does not change the condition of a people until they change it themselves" (13:11). This is similar to a famous English expression, "God helps those who help themselves."

Responsibilities during Occultation

It is, therefore, not enough for followers of *Ahl al-Bayt* (the Prophet's infallible progeny) to merely think about, and/or pray for the reappearance of Imam al-Mahdi during this period of occultation. Al-Mahdi's revolution seeks to found a global community, under one God, one religion, one system of law, and one ruler. For the achievement of this goal, the desire for such a revolution has to emanate from the people themselves. They have to actively prepare the ground for the commencement of Imam's revolution.

The process begins with self-development and self-purification. Islam abhors a stationary posture. As Imam Musa al-Kazim (a), the Seventh Imam in the line of succession to the Prophet, has said, Allah dislikes us being at the same point in our moral and ethical development today as we were yesterday, or to be at the same point tomorrow as we are today. Islam thus seeks to induce movement in us to achieve nearness to Allah.

The process continues by moving outwards, first, to include the local community and, then, to embrace the entire *ummah*. Islam expects us, to the extent of our abilities and resources, to make a contribution to the establishment of an Islamic public order with all its spiritual, moral, social and legal dimensions as well as to work for the well being and socio-economic betterment of the society as a whole.

A cynic might ask, "What if we prepare for the revolution and not live long enough to see it happen?" For, while the cumulative weight of individual "signs" of reappearance would suggest that the end of time couldn't be far, only Allah knows best the configuration of signs that would trigger the reappearance of the Imam. Imam Jafar as-Sadik (a), the Sixth Imam in the line of succession to the Prophet, anticipated the objection when he assured us that:

> "One who dies while expecting the government of al-Qaim [The Riser], he is like one who has been struck with a sword while accompanying him." He went on to amplify, "Nay, by Allah! He is like one who has been martyred in the presence of the Messenger of Allah [martyred in the sense that he would have died in the service of Islam]."

THE PROPHET'S STRATEGY FOR SOCIO-ECONOMIC REFORMS

Prophet Muhammad (s) was a revolutionary: he came to break the mold, not to fit into it. He was also, however, a realist: reforms cannot all be introduced at once lest the society degenerates into chaos. While the Prophet could not entertain any compromise on the necessity of making a series of reforms, he could, nonetheless, show pragmatism in the manner in which he implemented those reforms.

The challenge that the Prophet faced was to array social and economic practices of Arabia during the period of *jahilia* (ignorance) from those that are less inimical to those that are more inimical to Islam and, then, to correspondingly match his reforms to range, at one end of the spectrum, from:

§ revamping practices whose "form" could be retained but whose "content" had to be altered, and

§ regulating those that were being abused due to their excessive use, through, at the other end of the spectrum, to

§ phasing out practices whose immediate elimination would hurt the very people it was meant to help, and

§ abolishing those that posed a grave danger to the fabric of an Islamic society.

This essay will use one illustrative example of each of the four modes of reform listed above. It will, first, describe the rules and regulations that the Prophet, on the command of Allah (swt), instituted and, next, analyze the reasons for the choice of a particular mode of reform to ensure that, sooner or later, there is a complete and successful transformation of the structure of the society.

SOCIAL REFORMS THAT EXEMPLIFY ONE END OF THE SPECTRUM

Pilgrimage

Pilgrimage to Mecca, entailing the *tawaf* or circumambulation of the *Kaba* predates Islam and is an example of a socio-cum-religious practice that the Prophet converted into a purely religious rite. Following the time of Prophet Ibrahim (Abraham), the annual pilgrimage had gradually degenerated into naked pilgrims making seven circuits of the *Kaba* that had become the repository of 360 idols. Hence, it was a glorified type of idol worship that served both to boost the economic interests of the Meccan mercantile community and to enhance the nobility of the tribe of Quraish as the custodians of the *Kaba*.

When *hajj* or pilgrimage was introduced as one of the obligatory rites, Muslims initially mixed with the polytheists in making the *tawaf* of the *Kaba* (2:158). It was only after the successful conquest of Mecca that the Prophet, with the assistance of his cousin, Imam Ali b. Abi Talib (a), knocked down the idols and so purified the *Kaba* once and for all (17:81). And, it was only in the following year that a proclamation was issued that prohibited idol worshippers from entering the precincts of the sanctuary and so guarded believers from any relapse into polytheism (9:28).

Islam thus kept the ancient custom within the context of the Abrahamic tradition for, at the same time that the pagan pilgrims had used the *Kaba* for their idol worship, they believed that Ibrahim, the friend of God, had built it. As Dr. Ali Shariati has pointed out, while Islam retained the form, it completely changed its content. *Kaba* was now the symbol of the constancy and eternity of the One and Only Allah. The Arabs suffered no anguish as they moved easily from worship of idols to the unity of Allah, even though centuries of history separated the two antithetical purposes of *tawaf*.* The genius of the Prophet's strategy is that, more efficiently and successfully than any cultural revolution, he had undercut the foundation of idolatry and, in its stead, instituted submission to the Creator without the society realizing that it had left its past.

---

* Fatima is Fatima, trans. by Laleh Bakhtiar, 1980

Polygamy

Polygamy or, more accurately, polygyny, the taking of multiple wives contemporaneously, is an illustration of a social custom that was made more restrictive.[*] This custom was widespread not just among Arabs, but also among followers of monotheistic religions of Judaism and Christianity. There was no limit whatsoever on the number of wives a man had. It was, in fact, part of a much broader and deeper problem that looked upon women as mere chattels, marketable and transferable to others, with no legal rights or standing in society.

Islam sought to elevate the status of women centuries before the declaration of human rights by the United Nations. Within this broader agenda of inculcating deep respect for women and establishing their inalienable rights, the Prophet worked to curb the practice of polygamy. The Qur'an declared: " ... *marry such women as seem good to you, two and three and four."* The maximum was thus set at four. However, the verse immediately goes on to say that " *if you fear that you will not do justice* [among them], *then* [marry] *only one"* (4:3). A condition was imposed on taking more than one wife. This was, indeed, a very stringent condition for, in the terminology of the Qur'an, equity (*adl*) signifies not only equality in treatment in providing for the basic necessities of life, but also equity in love and respect. Absolute justice in the expression of personal feelings is well nigh impossible so the Qur'anic prescription amounted, in reality, to a prohibition.

Islam regulated polygamy so as to provide, as it were, "a safety valve" for any contingencies that might necessitate a person marrying more than one wife, or a society sanctioning multiple wives. An instance of the former situation is if the first wife turns out to be barren and cannot bear a child; an example of the second circumstance is if a war creates a huge imbalance in the ratio of men to women. The most fundamental point is that Islam regards the family as the basic organizational unit of the society. Hence, it wishes to incorporate within the family structure any person who might otherwise be left out, or reintegrate any person who happens to fall out of it.

---

[*] This section draws on Syed Amir Ali, The Spirit of Islam, 1981.

ECONOMIC REFORMS THAT EXEMPLIFY OTHER END OF THE SPECTRUM

Slavery

Slavery, taking of humans into bondage, is a case of an economic institution that the Prophet subjected to a gradual
change.* Just as with polygamy so, too, with slavery, the practice
was not restricted to the Arabian Peninsula. Its traces were visible in every region and in every age. Slaves were regarded as
commodities, to be acquired and exchanged at will. They were
used primarily for domestic help but also secondarily in the productive sector — to till the land, in seafaring activities, for public works, etc.

Prior to Islam, there were three primary ways in which persons
were enslaved. One was war in which the triumphant army could
enslave soldiers of the defeated army. Another was a chief or a
ruler who could enslave, at will, any person under his domin-
ion. Yet a third was a guardian who could sell, gift, lend, or
exchange his offspring in any manner he wished. Islam ruled all
these ways as illegal but for one carefully circumscribed excep-
tion. The defeated forces could be enslaved provided it was a
war of self-defense and the enemies were non-believers. Notwithstanding this dispensation, the Prophet introduced and enforced an alternative, *"set them free as a favor or let them ransom*
[themselves]" (47:4). In the first defensive Battle of Badr, the
Prophet set an example by freeing some prisoners without ransom, and allowing others to earn their freedom by teaching ten
Muslim children how to read and write.

Having sought to choke off the supply of slaves by ruling against
different ways of enslavement, the Prophet set out to undermine the institution of slavery itself. He declared emancipation
to be expiation of a number of sins, ranging from such serious
transgressions as failure to fast without a legitimate excuse during Ramadhan to such trivial violations as breach of a vow (58:3).
Lest it be argued that prescription of emancipation as penance
thus perpetuated slavery, Islam always offered another alternative for redemption of sins. Finally, the Prophet worked to both

---

* This section draws on Sayyid Akhtar Rizvi, <u>Slavery: From Islamic and Christian
Perspectives</u>, Vancouver Islamic Educational Foundation, Canada, 1972.

ameliorate the physical condition and restore the dignity of slaves. He enjoined masters to treat their slaves the same way as they would family members in how they were fed or clothed, and not to abuse or treat them unjustly (4:36). They could marry, appear as witnesses and participate with free men in all affairs. Most assuredly, Islam is the first and only religion that prescribed liberation of slaves as a virtue and an article of faith (90:11-13).

Islam thus employed a three-pronged approach to phase out slavery and, in the interim, to ensure humane treatment of slaves. It did not abolish slavery immediately not because of any concern for masters that their lifestyle would be affected, or that their economic condition would suffer. Rather, it did not do so because of fear for the fate of the salves themselves. Islam's strategy was vindicated when slaves were liberated overnight in the United States in the nineteenth century. Slaves gained their freedom but, alas, they were denied equality. They had to struggle long and hard to achieve a measure of integration in the larger society. It is sad that Islam's strategy of gradual emancipation of slaves was sabotaged when, under the Umayyad dynasty, slaves were acquired for the first time through purchase on the open market, a practice that shamefully continued intermittently through to the nineteenth century.

Usury

Usury, charging of exorbitant interest on money lended, is an instance of an economic transaction that was eliminated overnight. These dealings are still common even today in underdeveloped countries where non-traditional financial mechanisms (e.g., micro-lending) don't exit to provide the needy with small-scale loans without the security of a collateral. The practice was prevalent in Arabia before the advent of Islam as is evidenced by the fact that it was first prohibited in Mecca (3:130) but, because it evidently continued unabated, the Prophet was obliged to reintroduce the edict in Medina under severe warnings (2:275-281).

The Qur'an declared to the believers *"do not devour usury, making it double and redouble"* (3:130), underscoring its exploitative nature. The Arabic word for usury is *riba*, which literally means the growth of, or addition to the same thing. When the edict was proclaimed again, the Qur'an, to dispel any misconception, made a clear distinction between trade and usury — the former is a transaction that may yield profit but also involves risk, whereas the latter is an arrangement that, even in the event of default, the creditor can exact alternative forms of "repayment."

Islam prohibited usury outright because the consequences for those who have to default can be disastrous. It invariably leads to a vicious circle: the debtor is unable to repay, so he has to borrow more money just to pay the interest. Ultimately, he may lose whatever other meager possessions he might have, or be pressed into servitude himself or his family indefinitely. It is a situation from which one cannot easily extricate oneself. The most telling point is that Allah considers usury to be an act of "injustice," a conclusion that the renowned exegete, Allamah Tabatabai, has come to based on one of the verses that prohibited usury the second time – namely, that if money lenders forgo interest on loans previously extended *"neither shall you deal unjustly* [with others], *nor shall you be dealt with unjustly* [by Allah]" (2:279).[*]

CONCLUSION

With any attempts to reform a society, there is always tension between idealism - insistence on principles, and realism - surrender to expediency. The Prophet resolved this tension with pragmatism - use of expedient means to uphold cardinal principles.

The poet, Edmund Burke, did not approve of wholesale dismantling of societal institutions by the French revolutionaries of the late eighteenth century so he dubbed them "the ablest architects of ruin." By contrast, we can marvel at the wisdom of reforms introduced by the Prophet of Islam in the early seventh century and honor him as "the wisest reconstructionist of *jahilia* practices."

---

[*] <u>Al-Mizan: An Exegesis of the Qur'an</u>, trans. by Sayyid Akhtar Rizvi

FATIMA IS FATIMA*

The title of this essay is borrowed from a book with the same title. The author of that book, Dr. Ali Shariati, wished to imitate a French writer who, having reflected on all that had been said about Virgin Mary, concluded that "the totality of all that has been said . . . throughout all of these many centuries were not able to sufficiently describe the greatness of Mary as these words, 'Mary was the mother of Jesus Christ.'" Dr. Shariati attempted to round off the epilogue of his book in a similar vein:

> "I wished to say, 'Fatima is the daughter of the great Khadijeh.' I sensed it is not Fatima. I wished to say, 'Fatima is the daughter of Mohammed.' I sensed it is not Fatima. I wished to say, 'Fatima is the wife of Ali.' I sensed it is not Fatima. I wished to say 'Fatima is the mother of Hasan and Hosein.' I sensed it is not Fatima. I wished to say, 'Fatima is the mother of Zainab.' I still sensed it is not Fatima."

> He goes on to say, "No, these are all true and none of them are Fatima. FATIMA IS FATIMA."**

Dr. Shariati's summation is appropriate. It implies that Sayyida Fatima (a), the daughter of Prophet Muhammad (s) is, simply, unique – there hasn't been a lady like her before, nor is there going to be one like her ever after. Her uniqueness derives from two very special roles that she played in the history of Islam.

Prophets' Partner in Living Islam

So as to understand Sayyida Fatima's role, it is necessary to appreciate the Prophet's mission. And, to grasp his mission, it is essential to recognize the paradox of the co-association of Allah's (swt) Oneness (*Tawhid*) with His Justice (*Adl*). Allah lays down the *sharia*, the code of conduct for those who accept these two cardinal principles, along with others, that make up *Usul*

---

* Published in Az-Zahra, Volume 6, Issue 2, New York, July 2005
** Ali Shariati, Fatima is Fatima, trans. by Laleh Bakhtiar, 1980

a*d-Din* (the Roots of Religion). The *sharia* makes it incumbent upon believers to carry out obligatory deeds and to shun forbidden acts. It may be argued that it is easy to legislate such rules and regulations but it requires commitment and self-will to comply with them. Now, Allah Himself cannot act on the *sharia* or, as the expression goes, live it because it will compromise His Oneness. Nor can He ignore that responsibility because it will undermine His Justice.

Allah resolved this paradox - a seemingly contradictory situation that is, nonetheless, true - by the appointment of the *Ahl al-Bayt* (the Prophet's infallible progeny). Allah declares in the Qur'an, *"Certainly you have in the Apostle of Allah an excellent exemplar [uswatun hasanah] . . ."* (33:21). Prophet Muhammad was thus sent as a model for humankind. The believers have to obey his utterance as they were the words of none other than Allah. Further, they have to emulate his behavior as this was the standard that Allah had set for humankind to achieve perfection. Briefly, then, the Prophet did not just convey the message of Allah, he also lived that message.

The Prophet could demonstrate how to live Islam in multiple roles. While he could not show the relationship of a son with his parents since he was born an orphan and his mother passed away in his infancy, he treated his foster parents, first, his grandfather Abdul Muttalib and, then, his uncle Abu Talib and his wife, Fatima b. Asad, as if they were his real parents. The Prophet could play the part of a husband because he was married to Bibi Khadija and, after her demise, to several other wives. He could act in the role of a father for, while all his male offspring died in infancy, his daughter by his first spouse, Sayyida Fatima, outlived him. Finally, the Prophet could exhibit his relationship with the public by his behavior with his companions.

The Prophet could play the part of a son, but not a daughter. He could act as a husband, but not as a wife. He could be a father, but not a mother. He could show how to associate with companions, but not with a maid. This is where Sayyida Fatima comes into the picture. She would complement every one of the roles of the Prophet and so be his partner in living Islam. Between the two of them, they would present a perfect model for humanity.

The most graphic testimony of Sayyida Fatima's role in this partnership is from the Prophet himself: "Fatima is part of my being." He was speaking of more than a biological relationship. The word *bid'atun*, innermost part, refers to the essence of the Prophet's existence, his *risalat* (Prophethood). Just as the body is non-functional without its "innermost part," so, too, the mission of the Prophet would be incomplete without Fatima, its "innermost part."

Link between Prophethood and Imamate

Towards the end of his life, the Prophet was instructed to de-clare at *Ghadir-e-Khum* (a place between Mecca and Medina where he addressed Muslims on the return journey from his last pil-grimage in 632 A.D.) that, *"This day I have perfected for you your religion . . . and chosen for you Islam as the religion"* (5:3). There would be no further revelation and, consequently, Prophet Muhammad would be the last of the prophets. The Prophet was further instructed to install his successor, "Ali [b. Abi Talib] is the master (*maula*) for whomsoever I'm the master (*maula*)." Henceforth, the goal would be to preserve the message of Is-lam and defend it against any misinterpretation or distortion. The institution of Prophethood was soon to come to an end and, in its place, the institution of Imamate was about to begin.

Even while there was a change in leadership, there had to be continuity. The linchpin in this transition was Sayyida Fatima as she was the only daughter of the last Prophet and the first wife of the first Imam. There was a visible demonstration of this connection between the two institutions of leadership by the arrangement of the party that came to *Mubahila* (to meet with a delegation of Christians in 631 A.D. to resolve the issue of whether Issa (Jesus) is the prophet or the son of God). Prophet Muhammad was in the lead. He held the hand of his elder grand-son Hasan (a), and carried his younger grandson Husain (a). Imam Ali (a) was at the back. In-between the last of the Proph-ets and the first of the Imams was Sayyida Fatima[*].

---

[*] Events of both Ghadir and Mubahila are briefly discussed in the section on Event-based Eid in the essay entitled, "Bases of the Festival of Eid."

Sayyida Fatima's position is not simply based on biological relationship. When Imam Ali's right to succeed the Prophet as the leader of the Muslim *ummah* was denied, and he was forcibly brought to *Masjid-un-Nnabi* (Prophet's mosque in Medina) to extract from him an oath of allegiance to the newly appointed caliph, it was Sayyida Fatima who came to the rescue of the institution of Imamate. Surely, Imam Ali would have refused to pledge the oath and, in all probability, an order for his death would have been issued. The Prophet's most loyal companions – Abu Dharr, Ammar Yasir, Miqdad, Salman - would undoubtedly have intervened and would likely have been killed. They might have thus delayed the Imam's death but would not have prevented it. Sayyida Fatima stepped forward and tearfully threatened to remove her veil. The Caliph, fearful of the consequences of such an unorthodox action, backed off from his demand and Imam Ali's life was saved.

However tragic the death of Sayyida Fatima was at the tender age of 18, Allah deemed it fitting that she should be the first to depart from this world after the Prophet, to complete, in a sense, the transition from Prophethood to Imamate. During her short life, though, she had prepared her two sons, who were to successively assume the office of Imamate, for the great challenges that they were to face and for the far-reaching decisions that they were to make. Imam Hasan, against the wishes of his close companions, displayed great courage in signing a treaty with Muawiya b. Abi Sufyan, who wished to accede to the leadership of the Muslim empire, so as to pave the way for his younger brother's revolution. Imam Husain, against the advice of his near relatives, chose martyrdom to arouse the consciousness of Muslims when Yazid succeeded his father, Muawiya, as the next ruler of the Muslim empire. The inter-related actions of the two brothers ensured the preservation of the purity of the Islamic message for posterity.

> Allah attests to the linkage provided by Sayyida Fatima in *Hadith al-Kisa* (Tradition of the Cloak). When the *Panjatan* (the "Pure Five, the Prophet and his immediate descendants)* were under the cloak and *Jibraeel* (Angel) inquired about their identities, Allah made the introductions in this way: "Fatima, her father, her husband and her

sons." Allah made Sayyida Fatima the referent for the definition of all lineal relationships.

Conclusion

The twin roles that Sayyida Fatima filled were of such paramount significance that her contributions to Islam had to be publicly and continuously acknowledged so that she may be remembered and honored for them. The acknowledgment came from none other than the Prophet himself. He used to stand up to greet Sayyida Fatima every time she came in his presence. Did the Prophet perform this gesture out of special regard for her daughter, or for her womanhood? It was for neither. Had it been for one or the other, his companions and successors would have surely followed that practice, since it is not just the words but also the actions of the Prophet that they, along with the rest of the Muslims, are instructed to emulate. None adopted that practice. Clearly, the reverence shown by the Prophet was because FATIMA IS FATIMA.

THE LARGER SIGNIFICANCE OF SAYYIDA FATIMA'S CHALLENGE OF THE AUTHORITY OVER FADAK*

The Scene

Sayyida Fatima (a), the daughter of Prophet Muhammad (s), enters the court of the First Caliph of the Muslim empire, Abu Bakr b. Abi Kahafa, with a retinue of women from her clan of Bani Hashim. They are all covered, head to toe, in a veil and sit behind a curtain that was quickly drawn. It was an extraordinarily unusual moment for a lady who did not usually make public appearances and who had even left instructions that, when she died, her burial should take place in the dead of night. Furthermore, the court was held in the same mosque in Medina in Saudi Arabia where her father, the Prophet of Islam, led the daily congregational prayers and presided over the Muslim *ummah* or community. She was not, however, left with any other option.

The state had confiscated the estate of Fadak that was her own personal property. She had previously lodged a complaint that the Prophet had gifted it to her during his lifetime. She offered witnesses in support of her claim. The Caliph dismissed them as inadequate or unacceptable. She next reasoned that, if the property was deemed to be that of the Prophet's, then she was, in any case, entitled to it as the sole heir of her father. That claim, too, was summarily dismissed. Now, Sayyida Fatima decided to challenge the Authority in public in a court where the state would be cast as the usurper and she as the victim. But why did Sayyida Fatima go to the extreme of mounting such a public challenge to the Authority when her own husband, Imam Ali b. Abi Talib (a), chose not fight for his rightful claim as the duly appointed successor of the Prophet?**

Was the Reason Economic?

Fadak was an estate in the fertile valleys of the hills outside Medina. Sayyida Fatima had actually leased the estate for the four years that she possessed it. She used part of the income so

* Published in <u>Az-Zahra</u>, Volume 4, Issue 2, New York, August 2003
** Details of the episode are described in Jafar Subhani, <u>The Message</u>, 1984, and Sayed Ali Asgher Razwy, <u>A Restatement of the History of Islam and Muslims</u>, published by the World Federation, London, 1997.

generated to provide for the basic necessities of her family. But she disbursed a larger part of the income to members of Bani Hashim who were in need of financial assistance. Did Sayyida Fatima, then, wish to preserve her source of income?

The family had managed to survive, before and after Fadak, because their needs were limited and could easily be met by the state stipend supplemented by wages that Imam Ali earned through his own labor. Moreover, the family never retained any portion of material possessions beyond what they absolutely needed and gave away the rest in charity. There cannot be a better testimony to the family's charity giving than the one recounted in the Qur'an in *Surah al-Dhar* (Time, 76). The family had vowed to fast for three days following the recovery of the children from illness. Just at the time of breaking the fast, a poor, an orphan and a captive knocked on the door on three evenings in a row. Each member of the family gave away the only loaf of bread with which they intended to break their fast. When a family could donate their only item of food at the end of a long day of fast on three successive days, surely, that family would be least concerned about any material possessions.

But, it may be argued, that Imam Ali had been deprived of a leadership position. If he were to fight for his right, he could use the income from Fadak to rally support behind his cause. After all, the mother of Sayyida Fatima, Bibi Khadija, had put at the Prophet's disposal her vast personal wealth in the cause of Islam. Could it be that Sayyida Fatima wished to recover the leadership for her husband and so needed the means to finance that campaign?

While Imam Ali always maintained that he was the rightful successor of the Prophet, he made a conscious decision not to press his claim because he deemed it necessary to subordinate his own personal interests to the larger good of Islam. He dismissed with scorn the opportunists who tried to incite him to fight by promising him that they would throw their full support behind him. At the time of Prophet's demise, Islam was still very much in its infancy and Imam Ali knew that any dissension within the ranks of the Muslim *ummah* would jeopardize the success of the Prophet's mission.

Or ... Was the Reason Political?

The Prophet had worked hard to make equity and justice the two cornerstones of the society that he had built in the city-sate of Medina. This had been a Herculean effort because these values were alien to the society in which the Prophet was born. Moreover, the womenfolk had even fewer, if any, rights before the advent of Islam. The Arabs previously did not have any compunction in burying alive their newborn baby girls both because they were viewed as an economic liability and because they risked undermining tribal honor.

Sayyida Fatima could not submit to the whimsical rulings of the Authority. Confiscation of Fadak represented a violation of her legal rights under the *sharia* (divine law), above all, rights of a woman that the Prophet had enshrined. This was the first such violation. It was rapidly followed by many others during the reign of successive rulers. When Imam Ali, assumed the leadership of the Muslim *ummah* he sought to restore many of the rights that had to do with equity and justice for his subjects. Sayyida Fatima's message to the *ummah*, then and now, is to stand up for one's rights however slim the odds of winning.

Sayyida Fatima also wished to make a larger, telling political point. In her address to the court, she cogently advanced her claim to Fadak based on inheritance by quoting a series of verses from the Qur'an. The Prophet had taught that the Qur'an is the ultimate authority, that statements in the Qur'an have precedence over any *hadith* or tradition. In countering the arguments of Sayyida Fatima, the Caliph fell back on a *hadith*. It is not important that the *hadith* was, at worst, a complete fabrication that no other companion could remember and, at best, a gross distortion that substituted non-inheritance of intellectual heritage for material wealth of the prophets. What is more important is that he argued contrary to the juridical hierarchy that the Prophet had established and gave precedence to *hadith* over the Qur'an.

Thus, in a real sense, Sayyida Fatima demonstrated the wisdom of the parting advice from the Prophet (recorded on four separate occasions all within 90 days of his demise) contained in the famous *Hadith al-Thaqalayn* (Tradition of Two Precious Things). The Prophet had declared:

> "Verily, I am leaving behind two precious things:
> the Book of God and my kindred [*itrah*], my
> household [*Ahl al-Bayt*, the Prophet's infallible
> progeny], for indeed, the two will never separate
> until they come back to me by the Pond [of *al-
> Kawthar* on the Day of Judgment]."

Some dissenters had contended that the Qur'an was adequate
for them as a basis for guidance and that they did not need the
true interpretation and keen insights that only the Imams could
provide as the legitimate successors of the Prophet. Its is hugely
ironic that Sayyida Fatima depended on the Qur'an to make her
case, a book that was supposedly adequate in and of itself for
guidance, whereas the Caliph relied on a *hadith* to refute that
case, a source that was discounted as superfluous. Hence,
Sayyida Fatima's challenge had the effect of vindicating the
Prophet's *hadith* that inextricably linked the Qur'an to the *Ahl
al-Bayt*.

Compelling Proof

The primacy of political over economic reason for the challenge is underscored by later events. When Imam Ali assumed
the leadership of the Muslim empire after more than two decades, he sought to redress previous acts of inequities and in-
justices as mentioned above. He could very well, therefore, have
restored the estate of Fadak to the heirs of Sayyida Fatima.
Indeed, Fadak changed hands many times thereafter as one
Umayyad or Abbasid ruler returned it to the offspring of Sayyida
Fatima only to have another ruler from the same dynasties snatch
it back. Imam Ali, however, did not reverse the First Caliph's
verdict. The reason was simple: Fadak was not important for its
material worth, rather, it was significant for its symbolic value
as the first instance of a systematic violation of individual as
well as societal rights proclaimed by the Qur'an.

A full century later, Harun al-Rashid, an Abbasid ruler, asked
Imam Musa al-Kazim (a), the Seventh Imam in the line of succession to the Prophet, to indicate the boundaries of Fadak os-
tensibly with a view to restore it to the descendants of Sayyida
Fatima. The Imam retorted that Harun would not want to know
but, when he persisted, the Imam named the four corners of the
Muslim empire as the aerial extent of Fadak. Just as his grand-

father, Imam Ali, had suggested by his inaction so, too, the grandson intimated by his assertion that Fadak did not represent just a few acres of land, instead, it epitomized the extent of authority that should have been exercised by the legitimate successors of the Prophet.

WHAT MAKES A LEADER GREAT?
THE EXAMPLE OF IMAM ALI*

When we seek to seriously assess the greatness of a leader, a common approach is to identify a set of criteria and, then, evaluate the performance of that leader against that set. However, in setting up the criteria, we need to be cognizant of the position that a leader occupies and to tailor the criteria to address the specific functions that are associated with that position.

The first Imam, Imam Ali b. Abi Talib (a), assumed the leadership of the Muslim *ummah* or community a couple of dozen years after the demise of Prophet Muhammad (s), so this essay is concerned with his tenure as a politico-religious leader, in other words, as a leader of a theocracy from 656 to 661 A.D.** While there are many possible criteria that can be enumerated for such a leadership position, we will confine ourselves here to four, more important requirements that determine if a leader is truly great.

Criterion 1: Show Concern for the Larger Good, Not for One's Own Self Interest

The Prophet had declared Imam Ali as his successor at *Dhul Asheera* (the occasion when the Prophet invited elders of the community to publicly proclaim his mission in 610 A.D.), at the start of his prophetic mission. He installed him as his successor at *Ghadir-e-Khum* (a place between Mecca and Medina where he addressed Muslims on the return journey from his last pilgrimage in 632 A.D.), at the end of his mission. During the interim, the Prophet had underscored, both through his words and his actions, the complete line of succession.

However, on the demise of the Prophet, the Imam was denied his rights. It was painful for him to accept this situation, as is clear from the alternatives that he describes he faced in his famous sermon of *Ash-Shaq Shiqiyya* (recorded in *Nahj al-Balagha*):

* Published in Az-Zahra, Volume 3, Issue 3, New York, November 2002
** Murtaza Mutahhari, Polarization around the Character of Ali ibn Abi Talib, 1981; Sulayman Kattani, Imam Ali, trans. by I.K.A. Howerd, Islamic Education Center, Potomac, 1983

"There were two alternatives before me: either
to fight for my rights . . . or to patiently endure
the bereavement .... After having weighed the
situation carefully, I came to the conclusion that
the wisest course . . . was to face the disaster
with patience . . .."

The Imam reasoned that if he were to fight for the rights that
were bestowed upon him by Allah (swt), through the agency of
His Prophet, that he would risk a civil war amongst fellow Muslims. Such an outcome would, doubtless, lead to the destruction of Islam itself, which was still very much in its infancy.

It is this concern for the larger good of the Muslim *ummah* that
compelled Imam Ali to endure a long period of seclusion from
public life. He eloquently expressed his lofty principle thus:

" I will submit as long as the affairs of the Muslims
remain intact. I accept injustice only when it is
aimed against me alone."

Criterion 2: Govern Based on a Set of Principles, Even if they Put at Risk One's Own Position or Life

Imam Ali was driven by principles, not expediency. These principles, moreover, were based on divine wisdom, not his own
personal feelings or whims.

Within two decades of the Prophet's departure, there was widespread disaffection among the *ummah*. This led to a revolt that
resulted in the death of the third Caliph, Uthman b. Affan.
Drained and disillusioned, the *ummah* turned to the Imam for its
salvation. He was reluctant to assume the mantle of leadership
and, when he was finally persuaded, he coupled his agreement
with a blunt warning:

"You should know that if I respond to you, I
would lead you as I know and would not care
whatever one may say or abuse."

True to his word, the Imam remained indifferent to criticism of
his principled actions. He set about to reform the institutions

of government, and to purge it of powerful but corrupt officials. These officials resisted change fearful that their influence would be undermined if the Imam were successful in his reforms. They even raised a standard of rebellion on the pretext that he hadn't punished the murderers of the Caliph, even though no witnesses had come forward to identify the perpetrators. With a view to distract and weaken him, these officials forced the Imam to fight a series of civil wars immediately upon his accession.

The code of ethics that Imam Ali fully expected his new cadre of officials to embrace is enshrined in a letter that he wrote to Mailk al-Ashtar on his appointment as the governor of Egypt (recorded in *Nahj al-Balagha*):

a) Be kind and considerate, helpful and caring
b) Reduce the troubles and difficulties of your subjects
c) Do not oppress or tyrannize, do not abuse the power of your office
d) Do not ask of your subjects beyond their capabilities or power to provide.

Criterion 3: Uphold Equity and Justice for All, with No Regard to Any Distinctions

As the leader of the Muslim empire, Imam Ali retained for himself the right to issue stipend (monthly allowance) from the state treasury. His policy on distribution was rooted in fairness:

> "The wealth is Allah's. It will be equally divided among you, with no priority to any of you."

Even though this policy was extremely unpopular with the local elite, the Imam removed all distinctions hitherto made in the allocation of the stipend between Arabs and non-Arabs, and between early and later migrants into the newly established center of Kufa in Iraq.

The Imam's concern for the *ummah* was not just confined to the distribution of wealth. He also worked to give back man his dignity, and to recover for him his right to a free and honorable life. As he so poignantly put it:

"For me, the humiliated is not avenged till I secure his rights for him."

Criterion 4: Serve as a Role Model for All in the Society

In Islam, man has two sets of obligations: one is to his creator, Allah (swt), another is to his creation, especially humankind. Imam Ali demonstrated, in his personal life, how these obligations should be discharged.

The Imam's philosophy vis-à-vis one's obligations to Allah is elucidated in the way he classified different kinds of worship:

> "One group of people worships Allah out of desire for reward [of heaven]. This, surely, is the worship of traders. Another group worships Allah out of fear [of hell]. This is the worship of slaves. Still another group worships Allah out of gratefulness. This is the worship of free men."

The Imam himself was clearly in the third category for, as a free man, he worshipped Allah out of deeply-felt love for Him: "I found You worthy of worshipping," he declared, "so I worship You."

Imam Ali's approach to his relationship with his subjects is best described by what bin Dirar later told Muawiya b. Abi Sufyan after he had maneuvered to become the ruler of the Muslim empire:

> "By Allah, he was among us, *as one of us*."

Dirar had captured in that last (italicized) phrase an axiom that was later to become famous as "the government [read instead, the leader] of the people, for the people by the people." As Dirar himself went on to elaborate,

> "He used to answer us when we asked, receive us when we approached him, respond to us when we called him . . . ."

Conclusion

Even with just the four criteria discussed above, one is still left wondering how a man, who lived centuries before leadership had become a science that trains aspiring office holders to acquire the relevant skills set, could rise so far above the group of leaders pronounced great by historians. These modern-day leaders are invariably obsessed by their legacy, by how later-day historians will judge their performance in power. By contrast, Imam Ali could care less by what Orientalists or western scholars of Islam might have to say about the nature of his leadership. For, he was motivated, simply and purely, by one desire:

> To *earn* the pleasure of Allah to whom he had to return.

It can, thus, be truly said that the Imam was the perfect embodiment of this verse from *Sura al-Anam* (The Cattle):

> *"Say: Surely, my prayer and my sacrifice, and my life and my death are* [all] *for Allah, the Lord of the Worlds."* (6:162)

A PRINCIPLED OR A POPULAR LEADER?*

Dichotomy between the Elite and Public's Judgment

A president engages in an immoral, reprehensible act. He seeks to conceal his misdeeds by lying about them. The truth, however, emerges after an inquiry is launched into the affair. The president is ultimately compelled by the force of evidence to admit that, at the very least, he misled the public. Elected officials denounce the president's behavior and demand some form of retribution. The public acknowledges that the president's actions were unbecoming of the office, yet continues to endorse him because of his celebrated accomplishments.

The media decry the "disconnect" between the public's disapproval of his actions and their approval of his presidency, in other words, the distinction that the public makes between his moral character and his political leadership. An erstwhile politician, who is also a literary figure, bemoans this phenomenon in a book entitled, The Death of Outrage, that is, the failure of the public to express outrage at the shameful conduct of their leader.

The public has embraced an unprincipled president because he is a popular leader to the chagrin of the political elite. Yet it is ironic that, in passing their verdict on the reign of Imam Ali b. Abi Talib (a), western scholars of Islam known as Orientalists, have reversed their position and criticize him for refusing to compromise his principles for expediency.

Background to the Accession of Imam Ali

Before analyzing history's judgment of Imam Ali's leadership, it is important to first provide the background to his assumption of political office. The Seal of the Prophets, Prophet Muhammad (s), had proclaimed Imam Ali as his successor at *Dhul Asheera* (the occasion when the Prophet invited elders of the community to publicly proclaim his mission in 610 A.D.), right at the start of his prophetic mission. He installed him as

---

* This essay was written when President Bill Clinton was facing impeachment by the Congress of the Unites States. It was published in the souvenir publication for Imam Ali Day by Islamic Days Celebrating Council, November 1998.

his successor at *Ghadir-e-Khum* (a place between Mecca and Medina where he addressed Muslims on the return journey from his last pilgrimage in 632 A.D.), towards the end of his life. Yet, on the demise of the Prophet, Imam Ali's rights were denied. He painfully accepted the status quo out of his concern for the unity of the Islamic movement that was still in its infancy.

Within a little more than two decades of the Prophet's departure, the Muslim *ummah* or community fell on bad times. There was widespread disaffection and, when the then Caliph, Uthman b. Affan, would not heed the grievances of the populace, a delegation from the provinces that was in the capital to seek redress forced their way into his palace. The Caliph was killed in the melee that ensued. Drained and disillusioned, the *ummah* turned to Imam Ali in 656 A.D. He reluctantly accepted the challenge to bring the Islamic movement back on track, to restore the leadership that the Prophet had once provided.[*]

Imam's Model Leadership at the Governmental Level

The circumstances of his accession to power might have persuaded an ordinary leader to be cautious. Despite advice to the contrary, Imam Ali set about to reform the institutions of government, and to replace powerful and corrupt officials with apt and pious ones. These governmental officials, from the Caliph's clan of the Umayyads, sought to resist the change fearful that the influence that they had enjoyed would now be undermined if Imam Ali were successful in his reforms. They thus raised a standard of rebellion on the pretext that the Imam had failed to punish the murderers of the Caliph, even though no witnesses had come forward to identify any of the perpetrators. With a view to distract and weaken him, Imam Ali was forced to fight a series of civil wars, with the Muslims themselves, immediately upon his accession.

Yet the Imam did not flinch when a lesser leader might have. He aggressively implemented his plans of purging the government of unworthy officials and of expunging practices that were contrary to the Islamic letter or spirit. His code of ethics is enshrined in the letter that he wrote to Malik al-Ashtar, his ap-

---

[*] Mohammad Jawad Chirri, The Brother of Prophet Muhammad: Imam Ali, Islamic Center of Detroit, Michigan; Ali the Magnificent, compiled by Yousuf N. Laljee, Tahrike Tarsile Quran

pointee as the governor of Egypt (recorded in *Nahj al-Balagha*). He advises him to be kind and considerate, to be helpful and caring. Second, Malik should reduce the troubles and difficulties of his subjects. Third, Malik should not oppress or tyrannize them, abuse the power of his office. Finally, Imam instructs him not to ask of his subjects beyond their capabilities or power to provide.

Imam's Model Behavior at the Personal Level

As a leader of the Muslim *ummah*, Imam Ali had retained for himself the power to give stipend, a monthly allowance from the state treasury to the residents of the newly established capital of Kufa in Iraq. He took a step that was extremely unpopular with the local elite, namely, to remove the distinctions hitherto made between Arabs and non-Arabs, and between the early versus the later migrants into Kufa in the allocation of the stipend. Imam sought to be fair and equitable to all, regardless of their origins or status.

One day, Aqil b. Abi Talib, Imam's own brother, asked for more than his share of wheat from the state treasury. The Imam treated his family members and relatives no differently than he treated other citizens. As a matter of fact, he sought to educate and train them to follow his example and so, at times, was more severe with them than his other subjects. Thus, in response to Aqil's plea, the Imam heated a piece of iron on the fire and then brought it near him. He recoiled in fear whence the Imam said to him: "Aqil, you groan from a piece of iron heated by a creature for his sport, whereas you are dragging me towards a fire kindled by the Almighty for his wrath."

History's Mistaken Verdict on Imam Ali's Leadership

Notwithstanding numerous such instances of exemplary behavior in his public role and in his private life, the population of Kufa during Imam Ali's time was divided into three groups. One group consisted of partisans who were fiercely loyal to the Imam. Another group was made up of opportunists, tribal leaders and their hangers-on, whose interests were best served by a deadlock between the Imam and his principal adversaries (especially Muawiya b. Abi Sufyan, the governor of Syria). The masses of Kufa supported the form of leadership represented by Imam

Ali but they lacked the courage of their conviction. The times were such that they vacillated between the first two groups, alternatively supporting Imam Ali when they thought he would win, and deserting him when they feared he would lose.

History misjudged this political situation to pass a harsh verdict on the leadership of Imam Ali during the period of just over five years when he was the head of the Muslims. This is because history often confuses popularity with principles. It is willing to pronounce a leader as successful if his policies reflect the wishes of the people, regardless of whether those policies are right or wrong. And, it is equally ready to denounce a leader as a failure if his actions are rooted in a set of beliefs and values, irrespective of whether those actions are popular or not.

Imam Ali, however, was far from concerned about receiving a favorable judgment from later-day Orientalists. Rather, he was solely focused on earning the pleasure of Allah (swt), his creator, to whom he had to return. He put principles ahead of popularity.

WHAT WAS AT STAKE AT KARBALA?*

Karbala (the tragedy that occurred in Iraq in 680 A.D.) began with *Saqifah* (the event that happened in Saudi Arabia in 632 A.D.). Prophet Muhammad (s) had just passed away and, while his family was busy with the burial rites, some of his companions met at *Saqifah*, the assembly hall in Medina to plot their next move. They decided to bypass the declared successor of the Prophet, namely, his cousin and son-in-law Imam Ali b. Abi Talib (a), and to appoint one among themselves, viz, Abu Bakr b. Abi Kahafa, as the Caliph. This was a direct challenge to the leadership of the Imams from the progeny of the Prophet. How were they to react?

A Painful Trade-Off

The first point that should be stressed is that the successors of the Prophet, the Imams, were not concerned about themselves, only about the type of Islamic leadership and the welfare of the believers. Thus, while they repeatedly asserted their right to succession they, nevertheless, subjugated their own self-interest to the larger good of the society. Next, it should be pointed out that the Imams were put in a position in which they had to make a trade-off. This was, however, an unusual trade-off in that it was not between the better of two attractive outcomes, but between the lesser of two evils.

One set of considerations in the trade-off involved the nature of the theocratic state – the extent to which the Islamic state would continue to uphold the principles established by the Prophet. Another set of considerations in the trade-off involved the state of the Muslim *ummah* or community – the degree to which it would remain united in adhering to the religion taught by the Prophet.

The Imams had to make a painfully agonizing trade-off between these two sets of considerations. This is evident from the remark made by Imam Ali in his famous sermon of *Ash Shaqshiqiyya* (recorded in *Nahj al-Balagha*). The Imam says that he had two alternatives: "either to fight for my rights ... or [to] patiently endure the bereavement." After carefully weighing the alterna-

---

* Published in <u>Az-Zahra</u>, Volume 7, Issue 1, New York, February 2006

tives, the Imam chose the latter course even though it was "extremely painful and saddening" to him. The outcomes of the trade-off made by the first three Imams were all different because these considerations carried different levels of risk during the respective periods of their imamate.[*]

Outcome of Imam Ali's Trade-Off: Non-Resistance

The functions of the leader of an Islamic state, as enunciated by Ayatullah Behishti and Hujjatul-Islam Bahonar are four-fold:

§   Oversee all functions of government,
    including maintenance of law and order
    and administration of justice
§   Propagate Islam and expand its social and
    governmental influence
§   Engage in the exposition of the Qur'an
    and divine law
§   Serve as a role model such that people can
    emulate his behavior and attain salvation
    under his guidance.[**]

The first two functions require control of the political apparatus and so could fall under the purview of the caliphs. The Sunnis maintain that the caliphs share the third function with other companions of the Prophet and, indeed, they called upon Imam Ali to help them out in this regard. It could be argued, therefore, that they had the potential to perform two-and-a-half of the four functions.

The Prophet had established the city-state of Medina a mere ten years before his demise. True, during this period he had vanquished his Meccan adversaries and had broken the back of the Medinese Jewish resistance. True, he felt confident enough to look beyond the Arabian Peninsula and to invite rulers of neighboring states and heads of other religions to embrace Islam. Nevertheless, Islam was still in its infancy and a civil war would not only have divided the Muslim *ummah*, but also invited the erstwhile adversaries to regroup and challenge the Islamic state again. These fears were not unfounded as is borne out by events

---

[*] Details of historical events mentioned in this essay may be found in Syed Husain Jafri, The Origins and Early Development of Shi'a Islam, 1976.
[**] Philosophy of Islam, Islamic Publications, Salt Lake City

during the period of Imam Ali's own caliphate when he was forced to fight three civil wars and when the Umayyads used their base in Syria to challenge his leadership of the Muslim empire.

Imam Ali decided that it was not worth risking the unity of the frail *ummah* for an ideal theocratic state. Despite the encouragement of some hypocritical companions of the Prophet to claim his right to succession, Imam Ali decided to offer no resistance. He would, in fact, cooperate with the new regime whenever it was in the interest of Islam, but he would neither confer legitimacy to the political process nor to the three Caliphs who emerged as rulers from that process.

Outcome of Imam Hasan's Trade-Off: Negotiation

Imam Ali succeeded as the fourth Caliph in 656 A.D. Upon his death five years later, the governor of the powerful province of Syria, Muawiya b. Abi Sufyan, wished to wrest control of the empire from the proclaimed successor, Imam Hasan b. Ali (a). In a display of force, Muawiya immediately marched towards Kufa in Iraq, where Imam Hasan was based, with an army of 60,000. Simultaneously, however, he entered into a lengthy correspondence with the Imam. It is clear from this correspondence that he recognized Imam's closeness to the Prophet and his authority in religion. But he argued that he was best suited to provide political leadership and to protect the subject people. He thus conceded that the Imam was a superior leader, but maintained that he was a better politician. Muawiya, in other words, made explicit what was so far implicit, the separation of "church" and "state". Indeed, after the treaty had been concluded, Imam Hasan in his address to the Kufans made a distinction between a *"khalifa"* (caliph) and a *"malik"* (king). Muawiya himself often affirmed Imam's statement by declaring that he was "the first king in Islam."

Muawiya initiated peace negotiations because he did not wish to fight. For he did not just seek political power, but also legitimization of his authority. Imam Hasan entered into negotiations because he could not fight. For his commanders and foot soldiers had been lured away to Muawiya's army by rumors and bribes, and he could not be seen by historians to have turned down an offer of an unconditional peace from Muawiya who had invited him to stipulate the terms of the peace treaty.

Imam Hasan was thus left with no choice but to agree to a peace treaty. However, he sought to reverse both the ideological orientation of the state and the process of succession. One of the terms of the treaty that he laid down was that Muawiya would rule according to the Book of Allah and the *sunnah* (utterances and actions) of the Prophet, clearly implying that he had not hitherto adhered to these twin principles as the governor of Syria. Another term of the treaty was that Muawiya would not appoint or nominate anyone after him and, evidently, there was a tacit understanding that the caliphate would revert to Imam Hasan.

Outcome of Imam Husain's Trade-Off: Confrontation

Muawiya arranged for Imam Hasan to be killed in 670 A.D. He then violated a key provision of the treaty by maneuvering to have his son, Yazid b. Muawiya, recognized as his heir apparent. Imam Husain b. Ali's (a) hands were tied while Muawiya was still alive for he had to honor the treaty that his brother had signed. Only when Yazid succeeded as the hereditary ruler of the Muslim empire in 680 A.D. was Imam Husain free to revisit the trade-off.

While successive rulers purported to follow the dictates of the Qur'an, their interpretation of it was increasingly at variance with the teachings of the Prophet. While these rulers acknowledged *ahadith* or the traditions of the Prophet as the next most important source of legislative guidance, they increasingly sought to fabricate the traditions to support their own political agendas. To compound it all, Yazid, unlike his predecessors, had no use of religion and openly held its norms in contempt. Within half a century of the Prophet's death, a point had been reached where the survival of the true religion of Islam was at stake. So it is that in the will that Imam Husain left before his departure from his hometown of Medina for his ultimate destination of Karbala, he wrote that he set out to "**reform** the religion of my grandfather and of my father." He sought to redirect the *ummah* to the pristine, original Islam, away from the adulterated Islam that followed.

Imam Husain thus decided that confrontation with Yazid was his only resort. However, he chose not to confront Yazid with an army of soldiers, for historians would have undoubtedly questioned his motive. Instead, he decided to confront him with a band of martyrs, for the best way to rejuvenate the *ummah* was, in the words of the late Ayatullah Murtaza Mutahhari, to "inject blood into its veins."[*]

Conclusion

With the passage of time, the number of functions that an Islamic leader should perform had successively dwindled from four at the time of the Prophet (and briefly reinstated during the reign of Imam Ali) down to one during the time of Yazid. There had been a sea change from an exemplar, theocratic state to a despotic, secular one. The Imams, accordingly, had to ratchet up their response. There was now a shift from a passive policy to an activist one towards the official rulers of the Muslim empire.

Arabs had the age-old tradition of doing *bayya*, swearing an oath of loyalty to their tribal chiefs. The rulers used this tradition to ask prominent members of the community to swear allegiance to their regime. Abu Bakr, as the first Caliph, had the sense to waive this requirement for Imam Ali upon a threat issued by his spouse, Sayyida Fatima (a). He averted a crisis. Muawiya, as the founder of the Umayyad dynasty, had the smarts to avoid the need for asking for an oath from Imam Hasan. A crisis did not arise. Yazid, as the next ruler of that dynasty, was foolish to demand from Imam Husain an endorsement of his regime and to couple it with the threat of "or else." He precipitated a crisis. Consequently, Karbala had to happen.

---

[*] "The Martyr: An Analysis of the Concept of Martyrdom in Islam," in Sayyid Muhammad Rizvi (ed.), Imam Husayn: The Savior of Islam, 1984

MARTYRDOM: WHEN AND WHY?*

Concept of Martyrdom

Martyrdom is an alien concept to western thought and practice. At worst, it is seen to be a futile deed, one that does not accomplish any purpose. At best, it is thought to be an act that is intended to momentarily attract attention, to capture the headline. This misconception is further confounded by the fact that martyrdom is dismissed as an attempt by the faithful to buy a place in heaven. The ultimate reward is thus imputed to motivate the true purpose of the sacrifice.

On the other hand, Islam teaches that there is a time and place for martyrdom. This lesson was best demonstrated by Imam Husain b. Ali (a), the grandson of Prophet Muhammad (s) who, according to Muslims, is the last messenger of Allah (swt).

When is Martyrdom Called For

When Yazid b. Muawiya was appointed by his father to succeed him as the ruler of the Muslim empire in 680 A.D., contrary to the procedure that had hitherto been followed, he badly needed to legitimize his position. He, therefore, attempted to extract an oath of allegiance from key personalities of Islam, foremost among them being Imam Husain.

Basically, Imam Husain had two sets of options. The first option involved taking on Yazid, challenging his authority. He could have done this directly, by raising an army; indeed, the provinces of Yemen and Persia were known to be sympathetic to the family of the Prophet. Or, he could have done this indirectly, by stirring up a popular uprising; indeed, there was a movement in the offing in Kufa, a key administrative town in Iraq in the eastern part of the Muslim empire. However, there is no historical evidence that Imam Husain attempted to follow either of these approaches in challenging Yazid.

As Imam Husain saw it, the problem with this first option was that it depended on the use of military means against Yazid's

---

* Published in The Minaret, New York, June 16, 1993; reprinted in Az-Zahra, Volume 3, Issue 1, New York, March 2002

authority. Even if the Imam were successful in this venture, his success could easily have been misconstrued by the ruling dynasty's propaganda machinery then, and by western scholars of Islam since, as simply a political move to gain worldly power. His victory would thus have been temporary, short-lived.

The second option required that Imam Husain withdraw from the political arena and lead a passive life. Indeed, when he was pressed for an oath of allegiance, he migrated from one Saudi Arabian town of Medina to another one of Mecca where he lived quietly for several months. However, when the annual season of pilgrimage was approaching, he learned of Yazid's scheme to send some of his soldiers disguised as pilgrims with a view to assassinate him. He left Mecca for Kufa and, on the way, an offer of a safe heaven was made by Trimmah b. Adi at-Tahi to withdraw to the mountains of Tayy. He further promised that if the Imam so wished, or if it proved necessary, he would field as sizeable force of men to help the Imam. Imam Husain, however, declined this offer and continued with his journey. He was intercepted on orders from Yazid's commander and was diverted to Karbala, a town on the banks of the River Euphrates in Iraq.

The problem with the second option was that Imam Husain would have shirked from his ultimate responsibility. As the grandson of the Prophet, he deemed that it was his duty to prevent the complete destruction of Islam, which he feared would be the outcome if Yazid were allowed a free hand. He decided that the time had come for him to take a stand.

What is Martyrdom For

Imam Husain's goal was to bring about a complete revolution through arousing the consciousness of Muslims. His strategy was to achieve this through suffering and sacrifice. The Imam built these two planks into his strategy because he realized that sacrifice without suffering would be just as ineffective as suffering without sacrifice. He knew that victory attained through this uniquely powerful strategy would leave a permanent imprint on man's consciousness.[*]

---

[*] For the implementation of this strategy, see essays entitled, "The Station and Spectrum of Karbala's Martyrs" and " Imam Husain's Strategy for Karbala: Suffering the Sacrifice."

Evidence of Imam's grand plan can be adduced from the statements that he frequently made on the course of his journey from Medina to Karbala. Here, only two such statements will be cited. The first is right at the outset of his journey. Before leaving Medina, he wrote a will that he gave to his brother for safe custody in which he stated:

> "I'm not rising [against Yazid] as an insolent, or an arrogant, or a mischief monger, or as a tyrant. I've risen [against him] as I seek to **reform the *ummah* of my grandfather**. I wish to bid the good and forbid the evil, and to follow the way of my grandfather and father."

The Imam thus made it clear that he was not challenging Yazid as a person *per se*. Rather, he was rising against him for what he stood for as the leader of the Muslims. His purpose was not to punish him. Rather, his intention was to save the religion of Islam.

The second statement to be cited here comes towards the end of his life. Facing the army of Yazid in Karbala, Imam Husain said in his address:

> "O Men! Verily the Messenger of Allah has said: If someone sees a cruel king who permits those things which have been forbidden by Allah, who disregards His duty ... and that person does not do anything **in action or speech to change that situation**, then it would be right for Allah to place that person [on the Day of Judgment] alongside the tyrant leader."

The Imam clearly explains that the onus of changing an unjust situation is upon the populace. Indeed, if a person does not bestir himself in some way, then Allah would be within His right to treat that person no differently from the tyrant himself. Imam Husain recognized that he needed to change the situation that he faced, not just by his words but also by his action. He made a conscious decision to confront the oppressor and, in the process, lay down his life. He thus died a martyr.

Impact of Martyrdom

A martyr does not die in vain. His memory is perpetuated in the same way as the memory of other great men who have made their contributions to history and civilization. But the mode of perpetuation is quite different in these two cases. A scholar is immortalized through his knowledge, his books. An inventor is immortalized through his invention, his products. An artist is immortalized through his art, his paintings. An architect is immortalized through his creation, his buildings. But a martyr is immortalized in a unique way — through his blood.

The Iranian scholar, the late Ayatollah Murtaza Mutahhari, put it beautifully: "Martyrdom injects blood into the veins of society."* So long as the books of a great scholar are readily available in the book stores, or the products of a great inventor can be readily purchased in the retail stores, or the paintings of a great artist are prominently displayed in art galleries, or the structures of a great architect stand erect on this earth, their memories live on. A martyr, however, needs — nay, counts — on his followers to propagate his cause. Martyrdom does, indeed, arouse sorrow and passion in us. But for a martyr to achieve his goal, martyrdom must do much more. It must create understanding that, in turn, must generate commitment to scared causes.

---

* "The Martyr: An Analysis of the Concept of Martyrdom in Islam," in Sayyid Muhammad Rizvi (ed.), Imam Husayn: The Savior of Islam, 1984

THE STATION AND SPECTRUM OF KARBALA'S MARTYRS*

The goal of Imam Husain b. Ali (a), the grandson of Prophet Muhammad (s), was not to seize political power through the use of force, as is mistakenly alleged by Orientalists or western scholars of Islam. Rather, his mission was to revive Islam by raising the consciousness of Muslims, as is evidenced by his own statements made periodically from the beginning to the end of his journey, right from Medina in Saudi Arabia all the way to Karbala in Iraq.** To succeed in his mission, the Imam had to lay down lives in Karbala. It wasn't enough for him to sacrifice just his own life; he needed a "critical mass" of martyrs to have maximal impact on the Muslim consciousness.

Quality, Not Quantity

When Imam Husain left Mecca, his way station in Saudi Arabia in 680 A.D., it is estimated that he had with him about 50 persons who could bear arms, 18 relatives and 32 others. The latter number grew during the course of the journey (as well as after his arrival in Karbala when escapees from Kufa, another town in Iraq that had been blockaded, came to his help). The vast majority of the people who joined him, en route, were motivated solely by economic considerations, the expectation of material benefits should the Imam be triumphant over Yazid b. Muawiya who, as the heir to the Umayyad dynasty, had become the new ruler of the Muslim empire.

Yet, Imam Husain made it abundantly clear that there were no gains to be had, only sacrifices to be made. His most poignant message to his entourage came when he received the news of the death of his cousin, Muslim b. Aqil, whom he had sent earlier as his emissary to Kufa, at the invitation of that town's residents. Imam declared:

> "Our supporters have withdrawn their support from us. Whoever wishes to leave us and go his way, should do so."

** Published in Az-Zahra, Volume 5, Issue 1, New York, February 2004
** These statements are cited in the essay entitled, "Martyrdom: When and Why?"

At that point, it became obvious to everybody that the Imam would not fight Yazid, so it was futile to stay with him in the hope of any worldly rewards. Many, therefore, left him.

Having pruned the ranks of his companions, Imam Husain now set about to test those who remained. He tested *individually* some of his kinsmen as is evident from two such recorded instances. His intention was to test their resolve to die. Whilst still on the journey, Imam Husain narrated to his son, Ali al-Akbar, a dream in which he saw that they were all soon to meet their death.

> "Father . . . Are we not in the right?" asked the eighteen-year old son.
> "Indeed [we are]," he answered, "by Him to Whom all His servants must return."
> "Father," said Ali al-Akbar, "then we need have no concern, if we are going to die righteously."

On the eve of the tragedy, his nephew, Qasim b. al-Hasan, approached the Imam following a speech that he gave to his companions.

> "Will I also be among the martyrs?" inquired the fourteen-year old nephew.
> The Imam put it to him bluntly, "How do you see death?"
> " O uncle, death to me is sweeter than honey," replied the young Qasim.

As the hour of reckoning approached, Imam Husain tested his companions *collectively* in the speech referred to above. His purpose was to do a final check of their steadfastness. The speech is remarkable for its keen insights into human psychology. He first appealed to their reason – Yazid is only interested in his head so they should leave him to his own fate. Next, he relieved them of their social responsibility – he absolved them from the oath of allegiance that they had sworn to him. When all else failed, he protected them from a sense of shame – he put out the light so they could leave in the darkness of the night. None of the historians who recorded this incident mention that any companion left.

Before the battle was joined on the day of Ashura, Imam Husain had purged his forces and tested the purity of intention, alike, of his kinsmen and companions. They passed the test when they, in their own separate ways, assured him that they had made their decision according to the voice of their conscience and took full responsibility for their actions.

A Cross-Section, Not a Section

At the same time as Imam Husain encouraged some of his companions to leave him, he invited others to join him in his cause using whatever means he could to reach out to them. He dispatched a letter to his childhood friend, Habib b. Muzahir, who was a resident of Kufa. The letter intimated that if there was ever a time that the Imam could use his help, this was it. Habib promptly dashed to Karbala to arrive a day before Ashura. The Imam sought a postponement of the battle for one night on the grounds that they wished to offer prayers to Allah (swt). This stratagem gave the opportunity to Hurr b. Yazid al-Riyahi, who had intercepted the Imam at the behest of the enemy and diverted him to Karbala, to ponder over his fate. When he was convinced that the battle was imminent, he galloped across the line that divided the two forces to be with the Imam on the day of Ashura. He is only the most famous of reportedly thirty soldiers who defected from Yazid's army.

Imam Husain's decision to simultaneously trim and extend the ranks of his companions may, at first sight, appear odd. The explanation perhaps lies in his desire to not only ensure the quality, but also fill in the gaps in the spectrum of the martyrs he planned to offer. Only the Imam knows best the gaps he saw in his ranks, but we can point to the diversity that we observe in their demographic characteristics as well as in their personal affiliation and accomplishments[*]:

> With respect to age, the martyrs ranged from Aun and Muhammad, the children of Sayyida Zainab bint Ali (a), who were in their pre-teens to Muslim b. Awsajah, the companion of the holy Prophet (s), who was in his eighties.

[*] Profiles of martyrs cited in this essay may be found in Allamah Ali Naqi Naqvi, The Martyr for Mankind, trans. by S. Ali Akthar, Muhammadi Trust, London, 1986.

In terms of socio-economic status, the martyrs were arrayed from the chief of his clan, Habib b. Muzahir to the freed slave of African descent, Jaun b. Huwai.

In regard to political affiliation, on the one hand there was Abu Thumama al-Saidi, a partisan of Imam Ali (a), and on the other Hurr b. Yazid al-Riyahi, previously an officer in Yazid's army.

As for accomplishments, at one end there were men of literary distinctions, *huffaz al-Qur'an* (memorizers of Qur'an) and sources of traditions, such as Burayr b. Hudayr al-Hamadani, and at the other end men of military exploits, participants in earlier battles, such as Zuhair b. al-Qayn.

It may be surmised that Imam Husain sought a cross-section of martyrs for two reasons. He wanted history to record that it wasn't just one group or the other with some vested interests that stood beside him, but persons of every stripe recognized his cause as just and acted on their conviction. More importantly, he wanted future generations that would commemorate the tragedy of Karbala to be able to personally identify, at every stage in their life, with one particular individual in his lineup. His goal was not to promote *hero worship*, that is, imitation of the outward appearance and lifestyle of a person one dotes upon. Rather, his purpose was to facilitate the adoption of his martyrs as *role models*, that is, emulation of the inner character and values of a personality one admires.

So, how many of Imam Husains' kinsmen and companions became martyrs in Karbala? The late Maulana Sayyid Akhtar Rizvi painstakingly enumerated 120 names. However, we need to discount from his list those who died just before, or soon after Ashura and, perhaps, three more whose fate he indicates is uncertain. When we thus restrict the count, the number who died before the Imam himself on the day of Ashura is at least 106.[*] Yet, the number that is ingrained in every Shia's mind is 72. Why is there this discrepancy, then, between some 106 and 72?

---

[*] "The Martyrs of Karbala" reprinted in Sayyid Muhammad Rizvi (ed.), Imam Husayn: The Savior of Islam, 1984

A plausible explanation is offered by Syed Husain Jafri. Only 72 heads were taken to be presented to Ibn Ziyad, the governor of Kufa, and he suggests that the martyrs who were excluded did not have a tribal identity.[*]

Imam Husain went though a deliberate, purposeful selection process to present the best specimens of humanity on the battlefield of Karbala, persons who had attained a lofty station and encompassed a wide spectrum. There cannot be any greater tribute to Karbala's martyrs than the one paid by the Imam himself in that very speech on the eve of Ashura:

> "It is a fact that I am not aware of any companions more faithful and honest than my companions [including, therefore, companions of the Prophet and Imam Ali], and any relatives more righteous and kind than my relatives."

---

[*] The Origins and Early Development of Shi'a Islam, 1976

IMAM HUSAIN'S STRATEGY FOR KARBALA: SUFFERING THE SACRIFICE

Imam Husain b. Abi Talib (a) decided that the most effective way of bringing about the reform of the *ummah* or community of his grandfather, Prophet Muhammad (s), that had now become critically urgent was not through a political challenge to the Umayyad leadership but, rather, through a frontal attack on the consciousness of the subject people, the Muslim themselves. This required that he build two planks into his strategy of confrontation: suffering and sacrifice. For he realized that sacrifice without suffering would be just as ineffective as suffering without sacrifice. His strategy, therefore, can be summed up in three words: "suffering the sacrifice."* It is this potent combination that would infuse passion in his cause and bestir the *ummah* into action.

He, therefore, came to Karbala in Iraq ready and willing to lay down not just his own life, but also those of his relatives and companions so he could achieve a "critical mass." However, for martyrdom to have maximal impact, he needed to go further. He had to set the enemy up to inflict unwarranted suffering. The set up was designed to lead to violations at two levels – at the level of humanity, and at the level of the believers.**

VIOLATIONS OF FUNDAMENTAL HUMAN RIGHTS

Two examples will be cited that are intended to show how Imam Husain gave the enemy an opportunity to show their respect or, alternatively, disregard for certain basic human rights that are universally acknowledged as such from time immemorial.

Denial of Access to Water

When Imam Husain first arrived in Karbala on the second of *Muharram* (the first month of the Muslim calendar) in the year 680 A.D., he pitched his tents near the source of water, namely, River Euphrates. Five days later, when the forces of Yazid b.

---

* This phrase was first used by Allamah Ali Naqi Naqvi, The Martyr of Mankind, trans. by S. Ali Akthar, Muhammadi Trust, London, 1986.
** The violations mentioned in this essay are described in detail in S. Mir Ahmed Ali, Husain: The Savior of Islam, Tarikhe Tarsile Quran, New York, 1964.

Muawiya, the ruler of the Umayyad dynasty, began to pour in, they demanded that the Imam relocate his tents away from the river. Hazrat Abbas b. Ali (a), the brother of the Imam, was present at the Battle of Siffin that Yazid's father had fought with Imam's father, and he understood the perils of such a move. He had first-hand experience of the physiological and psychological effects of lack of access when the enemy briefly controlled the water supply at Siffin. He was, therefore, prepared to take a stand but the Imam sent word that he should accede to the demand of the enemy.

By the time of Ashura, the 10th day of *Muharram*, the Imam's side had been without water for three, long days. The elders bore the suffering with dignity but reporters of the events of Karbala recorded that cries of thirst could be heard from the children in the Imam's camp. Imam Husain decided to dramatize this flagrant denial of human right. He brought out into the battlefield his six-month old infant son, Hazrat Ali Asghar (a), to plead for water on his behalf. He tried to reason with the enemy that the battle was between them and him and that the innocent child should not have to pay for it. When Hazrat Ali Asghar next rolled his dry tongue over his parched lips, that action shook the enemy more than any other. The commander of Yazid's army, Ibn Saad, fearing a revolt, gave instructions to take out the child, and an arrow killed him in his father's arms.

Transgression of Private Property

The first act that Imam Husain performed when he arrived in Karbala was to purchase a piece of land from the local inhabitants. This land now became his private property so its sanctity had to be respected. However, on the morning of Ashura, Ibn Saad shot the first arrow across the boundary of the property and declared that, "Bear witness that I was the first to strike." He thus initiated the hostilities and the Imam was now forced to engage in a defensive battle.

Imam Husain registered his apprehension for the security of his womenfolk and children by, first, pitching his tents in a row, tied one to the other and, second, by digging a ditch at the back and lighting a fire on Ashura to prevent the enemy from attacking the encampment from the rear. Several times the enemy attempted or threatened to attack, but they were either pushed back or dissuaded from it. However, on the very evening of the martyrdom, in an act of glaring transgression, they invaded the encampment. Not only did they brutally rob the occupants of their meager possessions, but they also hurt their dignity by forcibly removing their veils. The enemy next torched the encampment and forced the women and children to spend the night in the open.

CONTEMPT FOR ELEMENTAL MUSLIM OBLIGATIONS

Two additional examples will be quoted that are designed to demonstrate how Imam Husain afforded the enemy the chance to honor or, alternatively, show contempt for obligations that are incumbent upon anyone who claims to be a Muslim, as did Yazid's forces.

Attack on Worshippers During an Obligatory Prayer

When it was time for noon prayers, Imam Husain requested time out from the hostilities in order to offer prayers. He directed two of his companions to stand in front of him so he could lead the prayers. A shortened form of prayers has been prescribed when under siege, called *salat al-khawf*. This is the first recorded instance of such a prayer being offered under a shower of arrows. One companion fell dead from the injuries he sustained as soon as the prayer was over. Another was hurt and, sensing that the enemy was getting dangerously close to the Imam, charged into their ranks and fell fighting.

Imam Husain exposed the enemy's hypocritical claim to being Muslims yet, again, when after a fierce fight, he could no longer maintain himself on his horse and came down to the ground. He then went into *sajda*, the most sublime part of the prayer when a worshipper prostrates before Allah (swt). Several of the enemies approached the Imam with a view to finish him off but retreated when they heard him entreat Allah to accept his humble sacrifice. Alas, Shimr b. Ziljaushan, stepped forward and slew the Imam in the state of prostration.

Disrespect for the Slain Bodies

Whenever a person fell in the battle, Imam Husain retrieved his body and laid it down near his encampment. The Imam neither had the time nor the resources to bury those who died on Ashura. Islam requires that the dead should be buried as soon as possible, preferably within 24 hours. It is an obligation upon the entire Muslim community to attend to the burial and none is relieved of this solemn duty until some come forward to perform the burial. When the battle ended, the enemy severed the heads of the martyrs and proceeded to celebrate their "victory," leaving the slain bodies under the open sky.

Imam Husain underscored, through the agency of Hazrat Ali Asghar, the depth of the hollowness of the enemy's claim to being Muslims. Of all the slain bodies, his was the only one that the Imam buried behind the encampment. When the battle was over and the enemy counted the number of heads, they realized that they were one short. Since they didn't know the exact site of the burial of Hazrat Ali Asghar, it is reported that they poked the earth with their lances in an effort to locate the body. They then raised his head on a lance, along with all of the other martyrs, to be taken on a long journey to Damascus, the capital of the Umayyad dynasty.

CONCLUSION

There have been many martyrs who have died for a cause they believed in. History has recorded their sacrifices and a few are even periodically remembered. Imam Husain is the only martyr in the annals of history whose anniversary is observed with the same fervor year after year. It is his unique sacrifice, accompanied with untold suffering, which arouses such intense passion in his followers throughout the world.

THE CHOICE FOR HAZRAT ABBAS IN KARBALA: DISPLAY BRAVERY OR LOYALTY?*

Hazrat Abbas (a), the son of Imam Ali b. Abi Talib (a), is famous for many outstanding qualities but two that particularly distinguish him and that endear him to his admirers are his bravery and loyalty. This essay will trace the roots of these two characteristics and then describe their inter-play in the tragedy of Karbala in 680 A.D., specifically, explain how and why Hazrat Abbas subordinated bravery to loyalty in the cause of Islam.

Roots of Bravery

After the demise of his first wife, Sayyida Fatima (a), Imam Ali decided to marry again but he desired a son that would be blessed with the genes of bravery. On the recommendation of a genealogist, a person who traces family descent, Imam Ali married in the tribe of Kalb that was distinguished for its chivalry. The woman he married was Fatima, popularly known as Ummul Banin, and she gave birth to Hazrat Abbas and three other sons.

Hazrat Abbas saw his first battle at the tender age of eleven at Siffin, the civil war that Imam Ali had to fight with Muawiya b. Abi Sufyan, the then governor of the province of Syria. A person appeared in that battle in a disguise. A famous Syrian fighter by the name of Ibn al-Shasa thought it was below his dignity to take on that person in disguise. He had seven sons so he sent one son after another as each was killed by that person. Finally, Ibn al-Shasa came forward himself to seek revenge for the killing of his sons but he, too, suffered the same fate from the same hands. When the person finally removed his mask, the enemy was surprised to see that it wasn't Imam Ali as they had suspected but, rather, it was his son, Hazrat Abbas.

> Abbas did in Siffin what he couldn't do in Karbala – he established his credentials as a great warrior.

Roots of Loyalty

The roots of loyalty go back farther, to the childhood of Hazrat Abbas. However, it was dramatically underscored on the 21st of

* Published in Az-Zahra, Volume 4, Issue 1, New York, New York, March 2003

Ramadhan (the 9th month of the Muslim calendar) when Imam Ali lay on his deathbed. He had gathered the family members together and then took the hands of all of them, except one, and placed them in the hands of his eldest son, Imam Hasan (a). He signaled with this gesture that, after his departure, Hasan was the head of the family. All had to follow his leadership.

The one person Imam Ali had left out was Hazrat Abbas. His mother, Janaabe Ummul Banin, naturally protested. At this point, Imam Ali summoned Imam Husain (a), his second son. He then placed the hands of Abbas in the hands of Husain.

> This exceptional gesture was a signal to Abbas that he was to take his cue from Husain, that he owed complete loyalty to him.

Imam Husain's Revolution

Before we analyze Hazrat Abbas's role in Karbala, we need to fully appreciate the mission of Imam Husain. A common mistake is to take a very narrow view of Husain's "enemy." It is implied that it was the person of Yazid, Muawiya's son and successor as the ruler of the Muslim empire. Doubtless, Yazid was a very evil, contemptible person. But, the Imam decided to fight him not as a person but, rather, as an institution that is an embodiment of Allah's (swt) Will on this earth. Muawiya had violated the terms of the treaty that he had signed with Imam's elder brother, Imam Hasan. This is because Muawiya maneuvered to ensure that Yazid succeeded him after his own death. Thus, it was after the separation of "church" and "state" finally became permanent that the Imam had to act to demonstrate Islam's insistence on a theocracy, a politico-religious order. Yazid just happened to be the best person against whom to launch the revolution. For, as Imam Husain wrote in his Will that he gave to his brother for safe custody before he left his hometown of Medina in Saudi Arabia:

> "I've risen [against Yazid] as I seek to reform the *ummah* [community] of my grandfather. I wish to bid the good and forbid the evil ..."

Imam's goal in Karbala was to bring about a revolution by arousing the consciousness of Muslims. He had a two-prong strategy: he set out to achieve his goal through suffering and sacrifice. For the Imam knew that victory through military strength would be temporary and, more importantly, his motives would be liable to be misunderstood. By contrast, victory through a frontal attack on the conscience would be permanent, and his motives could never be questioned.*

What Might Have Been at Karbala

Imam Husain had, among his followers, three of the bravest warriors in Arabia that he could have brought with him to Karbala. However, he divided his forces by design. He left his brother, Muhammad al-Hanafiyah, behind in Medina; he sent his cousin, Muslim b. Aqil, ahead of him to Kufa in Iraq; and he only brought with him his brother, Abbas b. Ali, to Karbala.

There were several incidents before the battle of Karbala when Abbas, if given a free hand, would have set the tone, would have demoralized the army. Once such incident was when the commander of the enemy forces asked Imam Husain to remove his encampment from near the River Euphrates. Another was when Shimr b. Ziljaushan approached Hazrat Abbas to win him over to Yazid's army. On both occasions, Hazrat Abbas wished to punish the enemy for their insolence but Imam Husain intervened to refrain him. History might well have been different if Imam Husain had a different goal.

What Actually Happened at Karbala

Imam Husain came to Karbala to lose the immediate battle but to win the larger war. His strategy is exemplified further in the manner in which he restrained Hazrat Abbas.

Every martyr of Karbala, except for those who were killed in the general attacks on the flanks of Imam's forces earlier in the battle, was given permission by the Imam to fight the enemy in one-to-one combat, as was the Arab custom in battle. Even the Imam's infant, six-month old son, Hazrat Ali Asghar (a), had the occasion to do so in his own unique way as he rolled his dry tongue over his parched lips when the Imam brought him into

---

* For the implementation of this strategy, see essays entitled, "The Station and Spectrum of Karbala's Martyrs" and " Imam Husain's Strategy for Karbala: Suffering the Sacrifice."

the battlefield to plead for some water for him. The only one who was denied this opportunity was Hazrat Abbas.

When Imam Husain had to finally send Hazrat Abbas into the battlefield, he came up with a novel idea to hamstring him. He asked him to fetch water from the River Euphrates, as the children had now been thirsty for three long days. He encumbered him not just with the water bag, but also with the standard of his army. Above all, he was equipped with a dagger, a defensive instrument, as opposed to a sword, an offensive weapon that other martyrs received when the Imam distributed the armaments to all his men. In other words, Hazrat Abbas was sent for a reason other than to fight.

There is no record of any instance when Hazrat Abbas questioned, let alone challenged the command of Imam Husain. He submitted out of his intense loyalty to his Imam. This was not, however, blind loyalty in the manner of an unthinking follower of a charismatic leader of a cult. Rather, it was informed loyalty of an insightful person who fully understood the larger good of his Imam's actions.

Conclusion

If you have it in you to change the course of history and you willingly agree to being held back so as to advance a lofty cause, that is a true measure of a great hero. Hazrat Abbas allowed his bravery to be dutifully subordinated to his loyalty and, in the process, elevated his status to that of a hero of Islam.

PAIRS OF PRINCIPALS IN THE PLANNING AND PUBLICITY OF KARBALA'S CAMPAIGN*

Karbala was a campaign. It wasn't that Prophet Muhammad's (s) grandson, Imam Husain b. Ali (a), was inadvertently trapped in an unfortunate situation that rapidly accelerated into his tragic death. Rather, once it became evident that he had to take a stand against Yazid b. Muawiya, the then ruler of the Muslim empire he, in a true sense of the word, orchestrated that epic event. His grand plan was to convert his certain death into a purposeful martyrdom with a view to having maximal impact on the Muslim *ummah* or community.

There were two phases to Imam's campaign, pre- and post-Ashura, the day of the tragedy in 680 A.D. The goal of the first phase was to arouse, through a potent mix of suffering and sacrifice, the consciousness of Muslims as Islam had been grossly distorted in the aftermath of the Prophet demise. The purpose of the second phase was to counter, via a powerful combination of integrity and empathy, the disinformation campaign that Yazid would mount to hide the circumstances surrounding the tragedy that occurred in Karbala in Iraq.**

A campaign requires careful planning and coordination. There were two principals who were primarily responsible for each phase of the campaign. During the pre-Ashura or planning phase, the pair consisted of Imam Husain and his brother, Hazrat Abbas (a). Similarly, during the post-Ashura or publicity phase, the pair comprised his successor Imam Zaynul Abidin (a) and his sister, Sayyida Zainab (a). Both pairs thus included the Imam of the time, and a brother or sister of Imam Husain.

Each principal in a pair had a unique role to play in the campaign. Their roles were consistent with their position and strengths. The Imams' authority devolved from their divine appointment and, accordingly, from their infallibility in decision-making. Their associates' parts were based on a key demographic characteristic coupled with a personality trait - in the case of Hazrat Abbas, on his physique and bravery that instilled fear in

* Published in <u>Az-Zahra</u>, Volume 6, Issue 1, New York, February 2005
** Events mentioned in this essay are described in detail in Ibrahim Ayati, <u>A Probe into the History of Ashura</u>, 1984, and Ayatullah Mohammad Yazdi, <u>Towards Karbala</u>.

the ranks of the enemy and, in the case of Sayyida Zainab, on her gender and oratory that commanded the respect of her audience.

PRE-ASHURA OR PLANNING PHASE

The roles of the pair of Imam Husain and Hazrat Abbas can best be appreciated by comparing them with those of the Chief Executive Officer (CEO) and the Chief Operating Officer (COO) in a major corporation. The CEO is expected to be a visionary, to set the overall business strategy for the corporation to achieve stipulated financial objectives, whereas the COO is required to be an implementer, to develop the tactics necessary to translate the business strategy into reality. So, too, with the pair of Imam Husain and Hazrat Abbas. As will be detailed below, the Imam was responsible for every major decision that began with his departure from Medina in Saudi Arabia and ended with his own sacrifice on the battlefield of Karbala. Hazrat Abbas had to carry out the decisions that the Imam had reached which sometimes required that he interact with the enemy on Imam's behalf.

When Yazid succeeded Muawiya, he pressed Imam Husain, against the parting advice of his father, for an oath of allegiance. He badly felt the need for legitimization of his authority. But, with the hereditary accession of Yazid, the separation of "church" and "state" that had hitherto been implicit now became explicit, so the Imam could not endorse the new regime. When asked by the governor of Medina for the oath, the Imam equivocated and decided to migrate from his hometown to the sanctuary of Mecca, both towns being in Saudi Arabia. He resided there for some four months and, only when he learned that Yazid had hired assassins disguised as pilgrims, that he decided to leave for Iraq on the eve of *hajj* or annual pilgrimage. Imam Husain could not allow the circumstances of his death to be shrouded in mystery; if he were to die, he would do so in an open field where right and wrong would be starkly juxtaposed for all Muslims to witness and adjudicate.

Once Imam Husain resolved to confront Yazid, he personally made a number of strategic decisions prior to his arrival in Karbala of which two will be cited here. When he left Mecca, he decided to take with him women as well as children of his household. Abdallah b. Abbas tried to dissuade him from leaving Mecca but, when he realized that the Imam was determined to go ahead, he counseled him that "if your trip is inevitable, then at least do not take your womenfolk and your children for, by God, I fear you will be killed." The Imam told him, as he told others who offered the same advice, "whatever is decreed to happen will happen, whether I pay heed to your advice or not." On his way to Kufa in Iraq, he was intercepted by Hurr b. Yazid al-Riyahi and, in the compromise that was reached on the route that he could take, the Imam ended up in Karbala. At the time of the encounter, Zuhayr b. Qayn advised the Imam that "fighting these people, now, will be easier for us than fighting those who will come against us after them." The Imam curtly replied, "I will not begin to fight against them."

Hazrat Abbas played the role of the implementer in chief. He made the necessary arrangements for the journey from Mecca and for replenishing supplies of provisions and water along the route to Karbala. He was also responsible for providing security, guarding the caravan against potential attacks by enemies and/or bandits. Hazrat Abbas' role was enlarged when the Imam later appointed him as the standard bearer of his small band in Karbala. He became responsible for making combat-related, operational decisions and for ensuring that the men who went out to fight were battle ready.

Upon arrival in Karbala, Imam Husain made a series of tactical decisions but two examples will be discussed here that demonstrate another role that Hazrat Abbas played, namely, that of a go-between with the enemy. It is not that Imam Husain did not speak directly with Yazid's forces. He did, indeed, address them before the start of the hostilities following the morning prayers and, again, just before he was killed soon after the afternoon prayers. These addresses were meant to alert the enemy combatants of the alternative choices that they faced and to warn them of the consequences of making the wrong choice. Otherwise, the Imam left episodic interaction with the enemy to his trusted brother.

Hazrat Abbas's role now was that of an emissary. The enemy demanded that the tents that the Imam's side had initially pitched near the River Euphrates be removed to a distant place so as to cut them off from the source of water. Mindful of the importance of the action that his father, Imam Ali b. Abi Talib (a), had taken to gain control of the river during the Battle of Siffin in which Hazrat Abbas had participated, he challenged the enemy at this demand. He backed off only when Imam Husain, wishing to sharpen the impact of martyrdom, sent instructions that he should accede to the demand. On the ninth of *Muharram* (the 1ˢᵗ month of the Muslim calendar) when the sound of an advancing army was heard in the camp, the Imam dispatched Hazrat Abbas to inquire about the intention of the enemy. He learned that they planned to embark on hostilities immediately if Imam Husain still refused to pledge the oath of allegiance. The Imam tasked Hazrat Abbas to negotiate a night's respite from the battle. While their domains for making decisions were thus different, the two acted in concert in much the same way as the CEO and COO dovetail their respective responsibilities.

Following the tragedy on Ashura, Imam Husain's grand plan called for a shift from a defensive to an offensive posture. Now that the sacrifice had been made, it was critically important that it not be in vain. Yazid would, surely, attempt to portray his actions in such a way as to protect his own position. The truth, however, would have to be told, even though the Imam's family members were prisoners with no freedom of action. Somehow, they would have to rise to the challenge and use unorthodox means to cut through the propaganda. In a manner of speech, the baton was passed on to the pair of Imam Zainul Abidin and Sayyida Zainab.

POST-ASHURA OR PUBLICITY PHASE

The roles of the pair of Imam Zainul Abidin and Sayyida Zainab are analogous to those of the Communications Director and the Press Secretary in a governmental administration. The Director has the overall responsibility of charting the communications strategy of the administration, deciding what the message should be and how it should be positioned to the wider public, while the Press Secretary acts as the mouthpiece, disseminating that message in the most effective manner. The same is true of the pair of Imam Zainul Abidin and Sayyida Zainab. As will be discussed below, notwithstanding the perception of a sick and frail Imam, he directed the publicity campaign and Sayyida Zainab, despite her more commanding presence, took her cue from him.

The most compelling proof that Imam Zainul Abidin was the leader of the post-Ashura phase can be found in the event that occurred on *Shame-e-Ghariba*, the evening following the martyrdom. When the enemy forces torched their encampment, Sayyida Zainab rushed to Imam Zainul Abidin to seek instructions on the course of action that she should take. Surely, common sense and Islamic injunction dictated that Sayyida Zainab should herself advise the women and children to evacuate the tents. However, she wanted it on the record that the Imam was the ultimate decision maker and household members did not emerge from the burning tents until he had given his decision.

Yazid had put out the word that the anonymous persons killed in Karbala were rebels against the regime since they sought to challenge the legitimate authority of the state. This was, however, the external justification that he offered for his brutal actions. For he also nurtured an inner motive that became evident when he addressed the *Ahl al-Bayt* (the Prophet's infallible progeny) in his court in Damascus in Syria. He wished to avenge the death of his forefathers at the Battle of Badr who had launched that attack in an unsuccessful attempt to destroy the mission of the Prophet. Imam Zainul Abidin and Sayyida Zainab had to formulate an effective strategy to counter this propaganda despite overwhelming odds.

Yazid had labeled the martyrs of Karbala as rebels. The first order of business, therefore, was to inform the public of the lineage of Husain. When Imam Zainul Abidin got a rare opportunity to address the congregation in the Mosque of Damascus, he introduced himself thus: "O people! I introduce myself to those among you who do not know me. I am the son of . . ." as he traced his descent from Prophets Ibrahim (Abraham) and Muhammad (s), through Imam Ali and Sayyida Fatima (a), to Imams Hasan and Husain (a). Yazid tried to silence the Imam by calling on the *muezzin* to recite the call for noon prayers, but the Imam turned the tables and delivered a killer blow when, on the mention of *"Ash-hado anna Muhammadar-Rasuloolah* [I bear witness that Muhammad is the Apostle of Allah]", he pointedly asked Yazid if "Muhammad was your grandfather or mine." This constituted the first fatal arrow in the quiver of the publicists of Karbala.

Yazid had implied that, as rebels, the martyrs of Karbala had questioned his authority as the leader of the Muslims. The second order of business, accordingly, was to acquaint the public that the actions of the regime were contrary to the teachings of Islam. When Sayyida Zainab spoke out in the court of Yazid, she told him, unequivocally, that he had deviated from the true Islam: "By what you have done, you have provided ample proof of arrogance against God, denial of His Prophet and rejection of the doctrines of the Holy Book and teachings sent down upon the Prophet by God." She went on to cite, as incriminating examples of his misdeeds, that he had "slaughtered and butchered the sons of the Prophet and imprisoned the members of his family." This constituted the second fatal arrow in the quiver of the publicists of Karbala.

While Imam Zainul Abidin and Sayyida Zainab placed different emphasis in their communications with the public, there was close consultation between the two as is the case between the Communications Director and the Press Secretary in view of the delicate nature of their functions. When Yazid was finally forced to release the prisoners in 681 A.D., he gave the Imam a couple of options. The latter first chose to consult with Sayyida Zainab before he gave his decision. She wanted access to a facility where she could gather the ladies of Damascus and recount the tragedy of Karbala, — in other words, initiate the institution of *majalis* in the very capital city of the ruler who had perpetrated the crimes against the Prophet's family. Sayyida Zainab would leave Damascus only after she could proudly proclaim to the *ummah* and to posterity, "mission accomplished."

Sayyida Zainab, who was in the forefront of the publicity campaign during the long, one-year plus ordeal from Karbala to Damascus, thereafter recedes into the background as Imam Zainul Abidin assumes a prominent role. It could be that she suffered from physical and emotional exhaustion, having had to take on the enemy at the same time as attend to the needs of her fellow captives. Or, it could be that having discharged her public duty, her priorities changed and she yearned to satisfy her inner desire of grieving, at long last, Karbala's martyrs. Thus it is that she advised the Imam to proceed from Damascus to Medina via Karbala. At the gravesite of Imam Husain, Sayyida Zainab must have had the great satisfaction of intimating that with the achievement of short-term triumph over Yazid, she would leave it to history to pronounce the long-run victory for Husainism.

FORMS OF WORSHIP IN ISLAM

Islam's fundamental goal for human beings is to induce movement in them over time. Allah (swt) abhors a stationary posture, where an individual is at the same point in his/her self-purification or self-development today as they were yesterday, and continue to remain at that same point tomorrow. Now, to assist human beings in making that movement, if they so choose, Allah has made obligatory certain religious practices. And He has decreed that, at the start of those practices, *niyya* or intention should be proclaimed with a view to remind worshippers of the purpose behind those rituals. *Niyya* includes the operative phrase of *kurbatan ilallah*, underscoring the fact that religious practices are designed to bring worshippers closer to Allah.

The obligatory practices are laid down in *Furuh ad-Din*, or the Branches of Religion. There are a total of ten practices and they cover two spheres of relationship with Allah: the first five have to do with *ibadat*, relationship with the Creator Himself, and the last four with *muamalat*, relationship with His creation. The sixth practice, *jihad*, represents the point of intersection between the two spheres because *jihad* is of two kinds — *jihad al-akbar*, which is the inner struggle against the forces of evil — an individual injunction, and *jihad al-asghar*, which is the outward struggle against invaders and non-believers — a collective injunction. This essay will focus on the first six practices to highlight the common theme that underlies them and to demonstrate Allah's compassion even as He makes these practices obligatory

Types of Sacrifices

The six religious practices are all quite different from each other yet they have one basic thing in common – they all require sacrifice of one type or another:

§ *Salat* requires the sacrifice of time since prayers have to be offered five times a day at intervals that begin from before dawn and continue after dusk (20:14)

§ *Sawm* involves forgoing, among other things, food and drinks during the fast, the basic necessities of life, from dawn to dusk for a period of a whole month, even though these items are allowed during the rest of the year (2:185)

§ *Hajj* demands sacrificing material comforts, changing the lifestyle that a person has become accustomed to, for a relatively short but very intense period during the pilgrimage to Mecca (22:27)

§ *Zakat* and *khums* require that a person pay a levy on a portion of his/her hard-earned assets or money to satisfy the needs of the less fortunate and to finance Islamic causes (2:43, 8:41)

§ *Jihad* may involve the ultimate sacrifice of life in a fight to uphold the principles of Islam (2:190, 9:36), or the difficult struggle of gaining control over powers (of intellect, anger, desire and imagination) that are inherent in one's own soul (29:69).

Human beings can make these kinds of sacrifices willingly only if they result from a conscious decision based on innermost convictions. That self-consciousness is necessary to lead to complete and utter submission to Allah and so to the desire to move nearer to Him.

Exemption from Sacrifices

These sacrifices are far from trivial and not everyone is in a position to make them. Allah has, therefore, provided grounds when a person may be excused from carrying out obligatory practices.* They appear to have been arrayed in order of excusableness in *Furuh ad-Din*, that is, acts that are rarely exempted are listed first, while those that are readily excused are listed last.

---

* The rulings quoted in this essay are from Islamic Laws, English Version of *Taudhihul Masae'l* According to the *Fatawa* of Ayatullah al-Husaini Seestani, published by the World Federation, London, 1994.

Beyond some general conditions that apply to observance of all practices (for example, attainment of puberty, sanity of mind, etc.):

§ External *jihad* becomes compulsory only when it is a war of self-defense, or when the Prophet or the Imam of the time (that is, after the 12th Imam comes out of occultation) commands it against polytheists, whereas internal *jihad* is rewarded for the effort but does not *per se* require recompense for lack of it.

§ *Khums* is paid on savings, not income so, unless a person saves enough over the course of a year, he/she is exempted from paying it.

§ *Zakat* is liable on only selected items of agricultural produce, heads of animals and coins of gold or silver that have legal tender when they exceed stipulated thresholds.

§ *Hajj* has to be performed by a person who has adequate money to pay for the cost of the round trip and associated expenses, and has enough left over to maintain his/her family for a full year after his/her return. However, if these conditions are met and a person cannot personally perform the pilgrimage because of ill-health, he/she has to commission someone else to perform it on his/her behalf during the person's lifetime; and, if the person dies before this obligation is carried out, it falls upon the heirs to make such an arrangement.

§ *Sawm* is obligatory if a person is in good health and is not traveling away from home. However, if a person misses any one fast because of these reasons, he/she is obliged to repay for everyone so missed but, if a person intentionally skips a fast, then he/she is required to pay back sixty fasts for everyone skipped (with the additional proviso that the first 31 fasts have to be continuous and, if continuity is broken without a just excuse, the person has to start all over again). Only if a person is permanently incapacitated is he/she totally exempted and, instead, has to feed 60 poor people to their fill in lieu of each fast.

§ *Salat* must be performed in a standing position. However, if a person is unable to stand due to ill-health, then he/she may stand with support but, if that is not possible, then the person may sit upright to offer the prayers. But, if that, too, is not possible, he/she may lie down first on the right side, next on the left side and, as a last resort, on his/her back and motion with the eyelids. Thus, so long as the person is conscious, he/she has to discharge the obligation of *salat*.

The fundamental point is that as religious practices call for a greater degree of sacrifice, so, too, the conditions for their observance are increasingly relaxed as is warranted by circumstances. *Salat* demands the least sacrifice but has to be offered under most situations; outward *jihad* requires the greatest sacrifice but is enjoined only under special circumstances while inward *jihad* does not *per se* involve requital for failure to engage in it. For religious practices that fall in between, the extent of their exemption appear to be proportional to the degree of their sacrifice. Allah, in His infinite wisdom and mercy, has thus ensured that a person's submission to Him is strictly in accordance with his/her capabilities.

ROLE OF RELIGIOUS PRACTICES IN FORGING SOCIAL RELATIONSHIPS

The Islamic code of life is customarily divided into two main spheres, or hinges upon two sets of relationships. The first is concerned with relationship with the creator, Allah (swt) – *ibadat*, religious practices that represent believers' expression of gratitude for His bounties and mercy. These practices are designed to bring them ever closer to Him. The second set has to do with relationship with His best creation, other human beings – *muamalat*, social interaction that arises out of their interdependencies. This interaction is intended to forge a caring and unified society.

This division is, however, merely for pedagogic convenience. Allah has, in fact, sought to inextricably link the two through the *sharia* or divine law. He has made acceptance of any religious practice conditional upon discharge of certain stipulated social obligations. This essay will examine one religious practice, namely, *salat* or daily prayers, that has been called the *meraj* of a *mumin* — *meraj* marks the ascension Prophet Muhammad (s) to the heavens when he came within "a measure of two bows or closer still" (53:9) to Allah, not in the sense of physical distance but, rather, in the sense of close communion with Allah. Even as worshippers come closest to Allah during prayers, He doesn't want them to be oblivious to their duties towards others; certain rules are enforced and other behaviors are encouraged that are designed to bring fellow believers together.

Concept of Congregational Prayers

There are five daily prayers that are *wajib* or obligatory. Every adult who meets certain conditions has to offer these prayers. Now, each individual can perform the prayers on his/her own. However, Islam introduced a concept in prayers that is unique among all regions. This is the concept of *salat al-jamaat*, or congregational prayers. Individuals gather to offer the prayers together in unison. A qualified religious leader, an *Imam*, leads the prayers and all others position themselves behind him and follow his lead. As the late Imam Khomeini so beautifully put it, "a congregational prayer is a manifestation of unity, brotherhood, friendship and affection which, without anyone being responsible for its order, itself has a spirit of discipline and order."[*]

The concept of congregational prayers is so dear to Allah that He has offered incentives to encourage Muslims to join in this act.[**] First, a person who performs prayers in congregation, earns manifold the *thawab* or reward of another person who offers it on his/her own (e.g., if there is only one person besides the *Imam*, one *raka* or unit, is equivalent to 150 *salat*; the equivalency doubles with each additional person up to a total of 10 persons; thereafter, the magnitude of *thawab* is known only to Allah). Second, more importantly, since just offering prayers does not relieve one of one's obligations unless that prayer is accepted, Allah guarantees acceptance of prayers of all who join the congregation if only one person's prayer is deemed valid. Thus, the larger the congregation, the greater the probability that prayers of all the worshippers would be accepted.

During the prayer itself, a person has to focus single-mindedly on Allah. However, certain stipulated rules or behaviors prior to, or immediately after the prayers lead to bonding among worshippers. One of the rules of congregational prayers is that there shouldn't be any gaps in the rows that worshippers form to perform their prayers. In abiding by this rule, a person has to literally rub shoulders with whoever is next to him/her. Upon completion of the prayers, a worshipper is encouraged to do *musafa* or shake hands with others to the right and left and, even, in front or behind him/her. Both these bodily contacts occur without any regard to the racial makeup or the socio-economic status of the nearest neighbors in prayers. It thus levels "the playing field" among the worshippers.

When congregational prayers are offered in a mosque, regular attendees get to know each other over a period of time. Thus, non-attendance of a worshipper for a sustained period is an indication to others to inquire about his/her well being, contact or visit him/her and provide any assistance necessary to relieve his/her distress. Furthermore, when a person from out of town joins the prayers, he/she is readily identified because of the requirement to pray *kasr*, that is, shorten obligatory prayers that

---

[*] Adabus-Salat or The Disciplines of the Prayer, 1996
[**] The rulings quoted in this essay are from Islamic Laws, English Version of *Taudhihul Masael* According to the *Fatawa* of Ayatullah al-Husaini Seestani, published by the World Federation, London, 1994.

consist of four *rakaat* to two. Hence, it becomes incumbent upon the locals to welcome the out-of-towner, extend their hospitality to him/her and offer any help that he/she might need in a strange city.

Incorporation of Scale in Congregational Prayers

So as to promote interaction with a larger section of the Muslim community, Allah linked congregational prayers to four scales or levels of observance. The first level is that of the neighborhood. Muslims are encouraged, whenever possible, to go to a mosque in the neighborhood to offer their prayers, rather than to offer them in their own homes. The *thawab* of a prayer in a mosque is a dozen times more than that of a prayer offered elsewhere. Furthermore, an *Imam* would invariably be leading the congregational prayers in that neighborhood mosque. Thus, relationships are forged with other Muslims in one's neighborhood.

The second level is that of a city block. Once a week, one of the noon prayers, *zuhr*, is replaced with *salat al-juma*, or the Friday prayer. This prayer is *wajibe takhyiri*, that is, a person has the option to offer *juma* or *zuhr* prayers. Unlike regular prayers where two persons can constitute a congregation, *juma* prayers require a minimum of five persons to form a congregation. More importantly, unlike regular prayers that can be performed in any mosque, *juma* prayers cannot be offered in two nearby mosques unless the minimum distance between them is about three miles. Consequently, relationships are now forged with a wider group of believers.

The third level is that of the city. Twice a year, on the occasion of *Eid al-Fitr* and *Eid al-Azha* (two festivals observed respectively after the end of the month of fast and the annual pilgrimage to Mecca), Muslims offer a *mustahab*, or an optional prayer. Of the myriad of optional prayers, *Eid* prayer is only one of two optional prayers that can be offered as a congregational prayer (while the other optional prayer, *istisqa*, for invocation of rain, is performed only on rare occasions). It is recommended that this prayer be performed in an open field so as to facilitate attendance by as many Muslims as possible. Hence, there is now the opportunity to forge relationships with residents of a large part, if not, the whole of the city.

The fourth level is that of the globe. Once in a lifetime, a Muslim is required to perform *hajj* or pilgrimage upon meeting certain requirements. This enables him/her to offer prayers in *Masjidul Haram*, in front of the *Kaba* in Mecca, for as many of the prayers described above as fall during his/her sojourn in that city. A person would have the opportunity to offer daily prayers for several days and, possibly, one Friday prayer together with other Muslims from all the different corners of the world in one huge congregation. Accordingly, possibility exits of forging relationships with Muslims from distant lands.

Conclusion

It will have been noticed that as the distance from one's own home to place of worship increases – first to the neighborhood mosque, next to the Friday mosque and to the *Eid* locale and, finally, to *Masjidul Haram* — the frequency with which prayers are to be offered also decreases — from several times daily, to once weekly, to twice yearly and, finally, to once in a lifetime. While Allah seeks to promote brother/sisterhood among the Muslim *ummah* or community, He doesn't want distance to be a burden on the believers in discharging their obligations to Him.

Prophet Muhammad likened the Muslim *ummah* to a human body and, to paraphrase him, when one part of the body hurts, the pain is felt by the rest of the body. A Muslim, therefore, has to be sensitive to the conditions of other Muslims throughout the world. This sensitivity should be manifest at two levels. At the cognitional level, a Muslim has to be aware of, and empathize with the situation of suffering Muslims. At the practical level, as in the specific example of *salat* described in this essay, a Muslim has to interact with, and inquire about other neighborhood Muslims as well as offer any help that might be required. The Muslim *ummah*, then, does not remain just an abstract, irrelevant construct, but it becomes a living, breathing reality.

IS THE ISLAMIC *SHARIA* FIXED, OR CAN IT EVOLVE?*

Like all other religions, Islam, too, has a system of beliefs or a set of principles. It also has a number of rituals or a set of practices that are based on those beliefs. But, unlike all other religions, laws promulgated to enforce those practices are not just confined to devotional acts. They extend to include all kinds of human transactions, be they personal, social, economic or legal. This is because Islam is not simply a religion in the ordinary, restricted sense of the word, rather, it is a complete code of life in an extraordinary, expansive meaning of the word.

Relational Spheres: *Ibadat* Versus *Muamalat*

Islam makes a fundamental distinction between two spheres of human relationships. The first is concerned with relationship with the creator, Allah (swt) – known as *ibadat*, these are religious practices that represent believers' expression of gratitude for His bounties and mercy. These observances are designed to bring them ever closer to Him. The second set has to do with relationship with His best creation, other human beings – referred to as *muamalat*, these are social interactions that arise out of interdependencies among human beings. This interaction is intended to forge a caring and unified society.

Both these sets of relationships are regulated by laws, the *sharia*. These laws have been deduced from juridical sources (the Qur'an and the *sunnah* or the traditions of the Prophet and the Imams) through the process of *ijtihad* (which also includes the exercise of reason (*aql*) and the consensus (*ijma*) of the early *ulama* or clergy). Unlike the Sunnis, the Shias did not feel the need for *ijtihad* until the beginning of the Major Occultation when their last imam, the Twelfth Imam in the progeny of Prophet Muhammad (s), was completely hidden from view. During the period of the Imams, however, Shias who lived in distant lands did not have easy access to their spiritual guides, so the companions performed *ijtihad* with the explicit approval of the Imams. This responsibility was subsequently devolved on the deputies of the Twelfth Imam, the *mujtahideen*, persons who, based

---

* Adapted from Our Marriage Ways: Will they Survive the Next Millennium? Published by the Khoja Shia Ithna-Asheri Muslim Community of Birmingham as part of the Silver Jubilee Celebrations, March 1998

on their sound belief and knowledge, are qualified to practice *ijtihad*.

Now, the laws of *ibadat* remain constant. Today, Muslims offer prayers five times a day, just as the Prophet did some fourteen hundred years ago. There may be a difference of opinion among the clergy about the status of the *juma* or Friday prayer, but both *juma* and *zuhr* (the noon prayer) cannot be simultaneously obligatory, as there will then be 36 prayers a week, not the 35 that have been stipulated. Similarly, Muslim fast during the holy month of *Ramadhan* in accordance with the command of the Prophet. There may be a difference of interpretation on whether an area has to "share the night" or be "united in the horizon" with another area where the moon was sighted before the festival of *Eid* can be celebrated, but *Ramadhan* remains no less than 29 and no more than 30 days. Hence, the basic configuration of devotional acts does not change, because Allah is eternal.

However, the laws of *muamalat* continuously evolve. For example, *fatawa* or juridical rulings become necessary for such financial transactions as payment of mortgage on a home, or purchase of stock/investment in mutual funds. Rulings were called for with new technological developments like the use of contraceptive devices to prevent pregnancies, or the practice of organ transplants to help needy patients. Thus, the rules that pertain to social, economic, legal and political matters evolve because the world constantly undergoes change. Indeed, the continued practice of *ijtihad* distinguishes the Shias from the Sunnis as having a dynamic and progressive faith that is equipped to address new issues as they arise.*

Confounding Influences: Religious Versus Cultural Practices

In the practice of religion, whether it is in the sphere of *ibadat* or *muamalat*, the *sharia* sometimes becomes embedded in the believers' culture, that is, cultural practices become intertwined with religious dictates. These practices are sometimes the product of the local environment, the socio-economic milieu in which

---

* See <u>Contemporary Legal Rulings in Shii Law</u>, 1996 and <u>A Guide to Islamic Medical Ethics</u>, 1998 both trans. by Hamid Mavani, and published by the Organization for the Advancement of Islamic Knowledge and Humanitarian Services, Montreal

118

they live. Other times, these practices are a function of the broader environment, the external influences of a dominant - in our times – western culture. Whatever the origin, whether internal or external, the effect is the same – the average person does not, or cannot, readily distinguish the tradition from the obligation.

Imam Ali b. Abi Talib (a), the First Imam in the line of succession to the Prophet, has intimated that cultural practices are not necessarily bad. In a famous letter that he wrote to Malik al-Ashtar on the occasion of his appointment as the Governor of Egypt (recorded in *Nahj al-Balagha*), the Imam warned: "Do not give up those practices and traditions and do not break those rules and regulations which good Muslims have evolved or introduced before you, which have created unity and amity among the various sections of the society and which have done good to the masses." The Imam was referring to more than just the traditions, but the twin criteria for acceptance applied equally to traditions: they should not contradict the *sharia* (implied by reference to traditions being developed by "good Muslims"), and they should be beneficial to the society (indicated by the use of the general phrase of having done "good to the masses").

It is essential, however, to make a distinction between two types of cultural practices. We can call the first type "accretions," customs that have nothing to do with religion *per se*. As the locale changes, or as the times change, old practices may be discarded and/or new ones acquired. Examples of practices associated, for example, with weddings of Asian Muslims residing in East Africa include ceremonies that are performed on the *bajot*, a small platform, that are obviously of Hindu origins going back to their roots in North-West India. They have survived in an attenuated form even in the new homes of those who have since migrated to western countries. Wedding ring and cake cutting ceremonies are imports from a pervasive western culture that were acquired during the colonial era in East Africa. They have, naturally, continued in their new setting in the West. These are accretions that can be dropped without any consequences.

We can refer to the second type of cultural practices as "enablers," customs that aid in the implementation of religious commands. These two are so closely interwoven that it becomes difficult to distinguish the dictate from the enabler. Illustrations of practices associated with devotional acts include the means of delivery of water for performance of ablution. It has changed from the use of a *lotto*, a utensil, to reliance on piped water, a washbasin. Determination of the sighting of a moon, too, has changed. There is now greater reliance on astronomical calculations as an aid in the process of sighting the moon. These are enablers that can change as conditions warrant.

Illustrative Example: *Hijab* Versus Partition

The need to separate religious from cultural practice and, further, to recognize whether a cultural practice is an accretion or an enabler is best illustrated with an example. *Hijab*, the Islamic modest dress, is unquestionably a religious decree.* "Partition" or separation of sexes by the interposition of a physical barrier in public gatherings, is simply an enabler. Reliance on the partition as a means of enforcing observance of *hijab* is, in fact, a practice that is unique among Muslims of Indo-Pakistani origin. This is not to say that partition does not serve other, perhaps, useful purposes. It is merely to recognize that, in its basic function, it is no more than an enabler.

Yet, unlike examples of enablers previously cited, the partition is arguably superfluous in the implementation of the religious dictate. Indeed, other Muslim communities such as Arabs and Iranians have, in their religious gatherings, separated the sexes into two sections without the necessity of a physical barrier between them. It is not inconceivable that partition may, in fact, have been used as "crutch" and so served as a disincentive in the observance of *hijab* in the first place. In other words, in an unusual reversal of the function, the enabler may have undermined the dictate itself.

---

* Murtaza Mutahhari, <u>The Islamic Modest Dress</u>, trans. by Laleh Bakhtiar, ABJAD, Albuquerque, 1988

BASES OF THE FESTIVAL OF *EID**

Eid is a celebratory event. Like any such other event, there is a basis or reason for celebration. There are four annual *Eids* that Shias celebrate. Before we explore the reasons behind these festivities, it is first necessary to make a distinction between two categories of *Eid*:

> **Self-based *Eid*:** The purpose of these occasions is to celebrate one self. These are: *Eid al-Fitr* on the 1st of *Shawwal* (10th month of the Muslim calendar) and *Eid al-Azha* on the 10th of *Dhul* Hijjah (12th month of the Muslim calendar). All Muslims, regardless of their denominations, mark these occasions.

> **Event-based *Eid*:** The purpose of these occasions is to celebrate certain events in Islamic history. These are: *Eid al-Ghadir* on the 18th of *Dhul Hijjah* and *Eid al-Mubahila* on the 24th of *Dhul Hijjah* (both in the 12th month of the Muslim calendar). Only Shia Muslims observe these two occasions.

Self-based *Eid*

Eid al-Fitr comes after the end of the fasting month, whereas *Eid al-Azha* follows the completion of the rites of *hajj* or pilgrimage. Both events, therefore, represent the culmination of what immediately precedes them. During *Ramadhan*, Muslims abstain from food and drinks as well as from sensual pleasures. These are items and activities that are permissible during the remaining eleven months of the year. In *Dhul Hijjah*, Muslims perform the pilgrimage to Mecca. This occurs under some of the most stringent juridical rules and strenuous environmental conditions. Both, thus, have this in common - they are a strenuous test of the body. The test, though, is different in emphasis — fasting is an act of self-denial, while *hajj* is a self-humbling experience.

---

* Published in Az-Zahra, Volume 6, Issue 3, New York, October 2005

The purpose of *Ramadhan* is to train the soul to resist what the body craves for even when these are perfectly legitimate desires outside of this month. This training is in self-control with the ultimate goal of helping believers move closer to Allah (swt). However, during this on-going process, one major obstacle that can retard their progress — or worse still, can force them to slide back — is the perception of one's importance or status. This perception could be fueled by one's pedigree, knowledge, wealth, or worldly success — in a word, one's ego. The purpose of *hajj* is to help believers conquer this ego so that they do not instantly destroy what they painstakingly accumulate over a long period of time.

Allah did not simply create human beings and leave them to fend for themselves. He gave them the Qur'an, the book of guidance, and He sent the Prophet, the infallible guide, to show them the right path. He could have, thereafter, left them to make their own choices. However, in His compassion and mercy, He tried to help them. He commanded believers to fast once a year because the soul needs a refresher course to restrain it from the ever-increasing temptations that surround it. He commanded believers to perform *hajj* once in a lifetime because one jolt to the ego may be all that is necessary to remind them of their humble origins and their final destiny. These are not impediments that He created for believers, rather, these are blessings that He showered upon them. Allah nudges believers along to assist them make the right decisions in life.

The festivals of *Eid al-Fitr* and *Eid al-Azha* begin with an offering of prayers to Allah. This consists of two *rakaat* of *salat*, or two units of prayers, in which, following *Sura al-Fatiha* (The Opening), *Sura al-Ala* (The Most High) is recited in the first *raka*, and *Sura al-Shams* (The Sun) in the second *raka*. There is one similar verse in both these chapters of the Qur'an that talks about the secret of success:

Kad aflaha mun tazakka
"He shall indeed be successful who purifies himself." (87:14)

Kad aflaha mun zakkaha
"He will indeed be successful who purifies it [the soul]*."* (91:9)

Allah promises that the one who will be triumphant will be the one who has mastered one's soul over one's body. The exercises of *Ramadhan* and *hajj* are designed to precisely achieve this and, following their successful completion, Allah wishes believers to celebrate those great feats of accomplishment. Even while they celebrate, Allah wants them to remember the less fortunate among them. Thus, He made acceptance of the fasts and *hajj* conditional upon them respectively paying the *Zakat al-Fitr*, giving alms, and doing the *Zabiha*, sacrificing an animal. That way, He ensured that the whole Muslim *ummah* or community could join in the celebration of *Eid*.

Event-based *Eid*

There are several events in Islamic history that could arguably be the basis of *Eid* but only two, *Ghadir* and *Mubahila*, are designated as such. *Mubahila* follows *Ghadir* by less than a week in the Islamic calendar but, in reality, *Mubahila* preceded *Ghadir* by less than one year. The former event occurred in 631 A.D., while the latter happened in 632 A.D. The reasons for both the importance and sequence of the events are intertwined[*].

Just as *Eid al-Fitr* and *Eid al-Azha* are linked so, too, the events of *Mubahila* and *Ghadir* are connected. The immediate reason or the "excuse," as it were, for *Mubahila* was to challenge the Christians about their belief that Prophet Issa (Jesus) is the son of God. Both parties were to do imprecation, invoke Allah to condemn the liars among them. But, in reality, it provided an opportunity for Allah to introduce *Panjatan* (the Pure Five, Prophet Muhammad (s) and his immediate descendants), as a group, to the Muslim *ummah*. Hitherto, the Prophet had merely talked about his household or had accorded special attention and/or affection to its individual members in public. Now, however, with himself in the lead, the Prophet paraded the five members of his household, in flesh and blood, in an open field for all to see and recognize.

Similarly, the immediate reason or the "pretext" for *Ghadir* was for the Prophet to deliver his farewell sermon, on his return

---

[*] Details of the two events may be found in Jafar Subhani, The Message, 1984, and Ghadir (Essays by Ayatullah Muhammad Baqir al-Sadr, Abdulaziz Sachedina, Sayyid Muhammad Rizvi and Husein Khimjee), published by NASIMCO, Toronto, 1990.

from the pilgrimage to Mecca, in which he foretold of his imminent departure from this world. But the Prophet used the opportunity to install the eldest male member of his *Ahlul Bayt* (the Prophet's infallible progeny), Imam Ali b. Abi Talib (a), as his successor. Previously, the Prophet had only declared, albeit repeatedly, that Imam Ali would be his vicegerent, though his involvement of the Imam in the discharge of the duties of prophethood served to reinforce his proclamation. Now, however, the Prophet conducted an investiture ceremony — unique in the history of succession of the Prophets and the Imams – once again, in an open field, for all 124,000 Muslims who had accompanied him on his last pilgrimage to witness and bear testimony.

The great significance of these events is attested by the fact that the Prophet was commanded by Allah to orchestrate them. The commands are recorded in the Qur'an itself:

> The command for *Mubahila* states: "*. . . whoever disputes with you in this matter* [of Prophet Issa {Jesus}] *after what has come to you of knowledge, then say: Come let us call our sons and your sons and our women and your women and our near people and your near people, then let us be earnest in prayer, and pray for the curse of Allah on liars.*" (3:61)

> The command for *Ghadir* states: "*O Apostle! Deliver what has been revealed to you from your Lord; and if you do it not, then you have not delivered His message . . .*" (5:67)

The transition from prophethood to imamate was meant to ensure the preservation and true interpretation of the final message. It was a watershed event. Allah wanted the *ummah* to take heed of it and be on guard against attempts to subvert His intention. Hence, the public introduction of, and the anointment of the first of the Prophet's successors have been designated as *Eid* both to rejoice in the honor bestowed on the Prophet's household and to beacon mankind to the right path.

124

Conclusion

Even though there are two categories of *Eid*, they are linked to each other at some level. Without the leadership of the Imams, the message of the Prophet would have been so distorted after his demise that the sacrifices of fasts and pilgrimage would have come to naught. They would have been degraded to acts of starvation and discomfort devoid of their deeper philosophical underpinnings. It is fitting, therefore, to celebrate both the divine institution of imamate and personal feats of accomplishment during *Ramadhan* and *hajj* that, together, help bring believers closer to Allah.

SYMBOLISM OF TWO CONTRASTING "MOVEMENTS" IN *HAJJ*[*]

Hajj, the annual pilgrimage to Mecca, is a deeply symbolic, if not also a very personal experience. This is to say that the rites that are decreed as obligatory in *hajj* have a symbolic significance that may strike different individuals differently. Now, the essence of symbolism is that there is a deeper, philosophical meaning behind the rites. On the face of it, the rites may appear as no more than devotional acts that are not related to each other. But, on reflection, they assume significance far beyond the acts themselves and reveal a depth and a connection that depends upon individuals' perceptibilities.

This essay focuses on two of the most important rites performed in *hajj* – *tawaf* or the circumambulation of the *Kaba*, and *saee* or the walk between the two mountains of *Safa* and *Marwa*. Both these rites are performed after seeking and gaining entry into the precincts of *Masjidul Haram,* the grand mosque in Mecca. *Tawaf* is performed first, followed almost immediately by *saee*. These rites entail movements that are in stark contrast to each other. It is the purpose of this essay to examine the likely philosophy behind the twin movements and to demonstrate the link between them.[**]

Circular Movement of *Tawaf*

The pilgrim joins the flow of people at the corner where *Hajar al-Aswad,* or the Black Stone, is fixed to the *Kaba*. He/she commences circumambulation by raising his/her right hand towards *Hajar al-Aswad* and declaring *"Allahu Akbar"* (Allah is the Greatest). During the circuit, he/she chooses to move along a path that keeps him/her within a stipulated distance of the *Kaba* (about 40 feet). The left shoulder faces the *Kaba* at all times as the pilgrim moves around it, but he/she is not supposed to touch the *Kaba* itself. The circuit ends at the same point where it began, at *Hajar al-Aswad*. *Tawaf* consists of a total of seven such circuits around the *Kaba*, one after the other, without a break. At the end of the seventh circuit, the pilgrim moves away from the flow of people just as gracefully as he/she first joined it.

---

[*] Published in <u>Az-Zahra</u>, Volume 3, Issue 2, New York, August 2002
[**] Some of the ideas discussed in this essay are drawn from Ali Shariati, <u>Hajj</u>, trans. by Ali Behzadnia and Najla Denny, Free Islamic Literatures, Houston, 1977.

Prior to the start of circumambulation, pilgrims pledge an oath of allegiance to Allah (swt). They affirm that any similar pledge that they might have previously made, to an individual or an entity, avowedly or tacitly, is henceforth null and void. Their submission to the Creator is absolute. The movement is circular around a fixed object. The object, the *Kaba*, symbolizes the constancy and eternity of Allah. The subject, by contrast, has a transient life. The course of the movement signifies total dependency on His being. The number seven perhaps designates the seven layers of heaven. They choose the specific orbit around Him, whether near or far, but stay within the confines of the *deen*, the path He laid down. They cannot, however, touch the *Kaba* itself for, even as they strive to move closer to Him, they can never quite reach Him. Further, they are not alone in their circumambulation. Rather, they are part of a larger group, the Muslim *ummah* or community, with whom they are both in physical contact and in a spiritual communion.

Linear Movement of *Saee*

Having performed the prayer of *tawaf*, the pilgrim moves over to an adjacent area to perform *saee* by joining another throng of people. The walk begins at *Safa*. He/she moves forward in the direction of *Marwa*. Around the middle of the walk, between the pillars of green stones, it is recommended to do *harwala* — for men to trot, and for women to quicken their pace. The walk ends at *Marwa*. As with *tawaf* so, too, with *saee*, the act is repeated seven times. Given the course and the odd number of walks, *saee* thus begins at one point and ends at a different point. The pilgrim is discouraged from resting during the course of a walk but he/she is permitted to do so between walks. On completion of *saee*, he/she performs *taqseer*, cutting off some hair or clipping nails. Thus ends the last rite of *hajj* and one is now free to remove *ihram* or the pilgrim's special garb.

The movement in *saee* is linear. It denotes constant struggle for existence, the need to cater to the basic needs of one's self and one's family. Sometimes, it is essential to strive a little harder than usual, to do *harwala*. Other times, it becomes necessary to take a major step and migrate, to do *hijra* from *Safa* to *Marwa*. Whatever the case, the direction of movement implies progress in the satisfaction of material needs. The number seven remains constant, underscoring the point that *tawaf* and *saee* are complementary and, hence, equally important in a person's life. *Taqseer* is a symbolic way to sever connections with the undesirable elements of one's previous lifestyle. As they remove their *ihram*, pilgrims are ready to start life anew, buoyed by the knowledge that they are joined by tens of millions of others who engage in the same daily struggle for existence.

Interconnection between *Tawaf* and *Saee*

Tawaf is performed in one part of *Masjidul Haram*, while *saee* is performed in another. The distance between the two areas, though, is relatively short. From one vantage point, one area is clearly visible from the other. *Saee*, too, follows hard on the heels of *tawaf*. Thus the two rites appear to be connected both in space and time.

Tawaf and *saee* have, in fact, been likened to the struggles of the soul and body respectively, to the upliftment of spiritual and material well being. *Tawaf* draws attention to the pains of "being," to the critical importance of preparing for life after death. On the other hand, *saee* underscores the joys of "living," the equally imperative need for full participation in life on earth. The body and soul are inextricably joined. Islam thus disapproves of the dichotomy between spiritual and secular obligations of mankind, just as it opposes the artificial separation of "church" and "state". For a Muslim, life is, in sum, a combination of *tawaf* and *saee*.

TWIN POLES OF AN ISLAMIC SOCIETY*

At one end of the spectrum of organizational forms is a human being, an individual by him/herself, and at the other end is the collection of all of human beings, humankind. Social entities that share a strong bond lie between these extremes of individuality and collectivity. Islam recognizes two such entities as the poles of the society. They lie nearer the two extremes: one pole is the family that consists of several individuals, and the other is the *ummah* that is made up of a large section of humanity.** These social entities are held together by natural ties. Islam, however, sought to extend their lineal and geographic limits respectively by introducing concepts that are unique at the same time as they are revolutionary.

The Family

The term family is not used in the modern sense of a nuclear family that consists of the husband, wife and their children. Rather, it is used in the traditional sense of an extended family that, in addition, usually includes grand parents and sometimes uncles and aunts.

The family in Islam comes into being through marriage between a man and a woman. Islam accords the greatest of importance to the institution of marriage. Prophet Muhammad (s) declared that, "No institution has been created in Islam more dearer in the sight of Allah than that of marriage." This emphasis is due to the integrating function that the family performs in society and, for this reason, Islam has spelt out the rights and obligations of every family member in order to ensure the preservation of the family structure.

Allah (swt) proclaims that, "of everything, We have created pairs" (51:49). This applies to all animate and inanimate objects, human beings not excepted. Thus, the natural basis of the family lies in the mutual attraction that Allah has created be-

---

* Adapted from Towards the Qur'anic Worldview. Report of the Los Angeles 2002 Retreat, published by IEB of NASIMCO, Toronto, 2004
** On the family, see Seyyed Hossein Nasr, A Young Muslim's Guide to the Modern World, Kazi Publications, Chicago, 1993; on the *ummah*, see Mahmoud M. Ayoub, Islam: Faith and Practice, The Open Press, Canada, 1989.

tween members of the opposite sex. When they join in matrimony, Allah goes a step further and puts between the spouses "love and compassion" (30:21) to cement that relationship. Love (*mawadah*) is nurtured by intimacy, and compassion (*rahmah*) grows out of companionship. Both lead to sympathetic consciousness of a partner's needs and concerted efforts to address them.

While these natural ties provide cohesion to the family, they restrict its extent. Islam sought to break out of the lineal limits by introducing a unique concept, that of *silat al-arham,* maintenance of the relationship of wombs (4:1). This is the relationship among those who are born from the same womb, or are related through various blood relationships. It is considered a religious duty to regularly visit and attend to the needs of kith and kin or, as the Qur'an puts it, to "join those that which Allah has bidden to be joined." (13:21). The opposite of this concept, *kat al-arham,* severance of the relationships, is considered an act of damnation (*lannah*) (13:25).

The *Ummah*

Ummah refers to a total community. From the Islamic point of view, humanity is one creation (2:213). However, human beings can find purpose and fulfillment in their lives only in smaller entities. As Allah declares, "*We have … made you tribes and families that you may know each other; surely the most honorable of you with Allah is the one among you most careful* [of his duty] …" (49:13). The purpose of these entities is to interact with, and enrich one another. They must compete only in their quest for the good and wholesome.

The Islamic *ummah* is formed through attachment to a single religion. The word is derived from the root word "*umm,*" mother; hence members of the *ummah* are children of one mother, Islam. The importance of the *ummah* in Islam is underscored by the belief that resurrection before Allah will occur with each humanity represented by, and standing around the prophet who is the founder of the religion followed by that humanity (17:71).

The natural basis of a community is the social nature of human beings. They tend to be gregarious and, ever since they progressed from being gatherers and hunters to becoming herdsmen and cultivators, they evolved from nomadic bands to sedentary communities. These communities exit at different levels, from that of tribes and clans to regional communities and nation-states. They are distinguished in terms of their ethnicity and/or language, and are sustained by common traditions and/or history.

While these natural ties hold together different organizational forms, they restrict their extent. Islam, again, sought to expand their geographical limits to embrace a larger section of humanity. It introduced another concept that is unique to Islam, that of *ukhuwwah* or brotherhood/sisterhood (49:10). This is the relationship that is formed by adherence to a common religion. This unity of faith, however, is not simply a personal commitment to principles and practices. It is a unity of purpose and destiny to create a society in total submission to the Will of Allah. Historical circumstances have, in the wake of the Prophet, precluded the realization of this ideal of a Muslim *ummah* and while no one, therefore, sees it in its fullness, every Muslim, nonetheless, inwardly experiences it.

Conclusion

The "natural" ties of attraction and gregariousness respectively bring together individuals and groups. To embrace a larger section of relatives and co-religionists, Islam, then, forges "acquired" ties through two unique concepts of the relationship of wombs and the sense of brotherhood/sisterhood. It makes acquired ties as powerful as natural ties by promising rewards for embracing these concepts and threatening condemnation for ignoring them. In this way, Islam binds together the resultant larger entities of all relatives and of all Muslims. It is this togetherness that the Prophet refers to in a *hadith* or tradition: "Togetherness is [a source of] goodness, and separation [a cause of] misery."

SYSTEM OF ISLAMIC JUSTICE AS ILLUSTRATED BY CRIMINAL LAW

Islam's fundamental goal for the society as a whole is the establishment of a just and equitable society. Thus, the Qur'an declares that Prophets were sent with *"the Book and the scale* [criterion between right and wrong] *so that mankind may conduct themselves with justice"* (57:25). The society would be based solely on the behavior of individuals in that the victim and the offender would both be treated fairly without any regard to their social status or position in the society. The law that would be enforced would be divine law that is influenced neither by the vested interests of the few, nor the personal wishes of the majority.

The focus of this essay is on criminal law that is concerned with the relationship between the individual and the general public. Islam recognizes two categories of crimes:

§ Crimes that jeopardize the well-being of the society, that is, crimes that undermine its moral and ethical fabric, and

§ Crimes that infringe upon the rights of individuals, that is, crimes that have an adverse effect on their person or dignity.

Islam deals with these two categories of crimes in a fundamentally different manner as will be illustrated with selected examples.[*]

PUBLIC WRONGS

The first category covers areas considered essential for the maintenance of public morality and protection of Islamic values. Here, the rights of Allah (swt) take precedence over the rights of individuals. Since Allah is the symbol of the Islamic community, these crimes are the same as modern legal system's conception of "public wrongs." The goal of punishment for such crimes is psychological deterrence. The *sharia* or divine law defines punishment and there is little, if any room for a judge's

---

[*] The discussion of these examples draws on S. Mir Ahmed Ali, The Holy Qur'an, 1964, and Allamah Sayyid Muhammad Tabatabai, Al-Mizan: An Exegesis of the Qur'an, trans. by Sayyid Akhtar Rizvi (1st 5 chapters).

discretionary powers. His/her role is limited to the assessment of guilt or innocence; if the guilt is established beyond a reasonable doubt, he/she has no alternative but to impose the penalty defined.

Theft

"And [as for] *the man who steals and the woman who steals, cut off their hands as a punishment for what they have earned, an exemplary punishment from Allah; and Allah is Mighty, Wise."* (5:38)

The severity of the punishment for theft has prompted many a western commentator to denounce it as far too inhuman. However, this law has to be understood in the context of the society that Islam envisages – that the basic needs of life are secured for every member of the society through the chance to earn a living under fair conditions, and that those who are temporarily or permanently incapacitated can rely on the system of social welfare financed through *zakat* and *khums* levied on the more fortunate members of the society. Furthermore, the traditions suggest that robbery has to exceed a certain monetary value before the punishment can be meted out. The overriding consideration of the decree is to ensure that there is complete law and order in the society so that all members feel safe and secure.

Adultery

"[As for] *the fornicatress and the fornicator, flog each of them,* [giving] *a hundred stripes, and let not pity for them detain you* [from carrying out] *in the matter of obedience to Allah, if you believe in Allah and the last day, and let a party of believers witness their chastisement."* (24:2)

Notwithstanding the translation of the above verse, the Arabic word *zina* refers to any sexual intercourse between a man and a woman out of wedlock and so covers both adultery and fornication. Since Islam regards marriage as the bedrock of the society and since it charges individuals, the family, the society and the state to facilitate it, it forbids any illicit sexual intercourse. The requirement that some number of believers witness the flogging is meant as an additional social pressure to deter others from committing such a morally corruptive offence.

INDIVIDUAL WRONGS

The second category of crimes covers violation of rights of individual members of the society. These crimes are the same as modern legal system's conception of "individual wrongs." The aim of punishment is to appease the victims and/or the nearest relatives. Punishment is designed to strike a balance between the harm caused by the offender and the severity of the penalty imposed upon him/her. A judge's role is to enforce the principle of proportionality – "and the recompense for evil is punishment like it" (42:40) – that is, punishment should be commensurate with the crime. However, the victim and his/her relatives now have a role in determining whether the sentence should be carried out or commuted.

Slander

"And those who accuse free [chaste] *women* [of fornication or adultery] *then do not bring four witnesses* [in support of the accusation] *flog them* [giving] *eighty stripes, and do not admit any evidence from them ever; and these it is that are the transgressors."* (24:4)

Slander involves making false charges that defame and damage another person's reputation. The Qur'an thus requires that four witnesses back up the accusation and, if it is not substantiated, a severe penalty is to be imposed to prevent any irresponsible or malicious behavior. In addition to flogging which is a degrading punishment in and of itself, the Qur'an prescribes yet another penalty that permanently ruins the reputation of the slanderer, namely, they are forever disqualified to appear as witnesses in a court of law.

Manslaughter Vs. Murder

" ... whoever kills a believer by mistake, he should free a believing slave, and blood-money should be paid to his people unless they remit as alms ... but he who cannot find [a slave] should fast for two months successively: a penance from Allah, and Allah is Knowing, Wise." (4:92)

"And we prescribed to them in it [the Torah] *that life is for life, and eye for eye, and nose for nose, and ear for ear, and tooth for tooth, and* [that there is similar] *reprisal in wounds; but he who forgoes it* [out of generosity and magnanimity], *it shall be an expiation* [for some

past wrongdoings] *for him; and whoever did not judge by what Allah revealed, those are they that are the unjust."* (5:45)

The Qur'an makes a clear distinction between unintentional manslaughter and pre-meditated murder. Beyond the payment of indemnity, the penalty for manslaughter of a believer is to free a believing slave. The only way to make up for one life that has been destroyed, the Qur'an intimates, is to give life back to another person, a slave, who has been deprived of it. This is just one of many ways in which Islam sought to end the institution of slavery, not to perpetuate it since an alternative recompense is prescribed in the event that there are no slaves left to be freed.

Western lawmakers have for the longest time advanced arguments for and against capital punishment for murder and both sets of arguments appear to be cogent and reasonable. Proponents cite the principle of justice or fairness, whereas opponents invoke the principle of mercy or forgiveness. Islam maintains that justice can be demanded and can, therefore, be legislated. Mercy, on the other hand, can only be pleaded for, so discretion has to come into play. Both principles are beautifully accommodated in the Islamic legal system: victim has the legal right for revenge, but victim or his/her relatives also have the moral obligation either to forgive the criminal or to settle for a monetary compensation. The wisdom of such a ruling can be readily appreciated in contemporary times as DNA evidence has conclusively proved the innocence of many inmates on the death row in what are clear instances of miscarriage of justice.

CONCLUSION

It is manifest from the examples of crimes discussed in this essay that Islam encourages forgiveness in individual wrongs but disallows leniency in public wrongs. The logic behind the legal standards laid down for these two categories of crimes leaves no doubt that Islam is a divinely inspired religion.

ABOUT THE AUTHOR

Dr. Bashir A. Datoo was born in Zanzibar, an island off the coast of Tanzania, and grew up in a family and a broader community that was imbued with Islamic ideology and steeped in its traditions. He attended a religious school in the evenings for several years to learn the fundamentals of Islam.

After he settled in the United States, Dr. Datoo became the principal of a newly established weekend religious school in New Jersey. During his tenure for nearly a decade, he introduced a curriculum that consisted of four core courses of Qur'an, *Aqaid* and *Fiqh* (Beliefs and Jurisprudence), *Akhlaq* (Ethics), and *Tarikh* (History).

During that time, Dr. Datoo became a key member of the Islamic Education Board of a North American Muslim Communities Organization. The Board launched a number of initiatives for weekend religious schools ranging from Curriculum Development Process to Drive for Excellence in Educational Program. He was also one of the principal organizers of its biennial retreats held between 1996 and 2004 and authored all of the proceedings.

Upon completion of his post-high school education in Zanzibar, Dr. Datoo proceeded to Makerere University in Uganda to read his bachelor's degree. Next, he went to the London School of Economics and Political Science of the University of London for his doctoral studies.

On his return to Tanzania, Dr. Datoo taught at the University of Dar-es-Salaam in the capital city from 1968-1976 where he rose to the rank of Associate Professor. On a sabbatical leave in 1972 and, then, in 1976, he came to Minnesota University in Minneapolis and Princeton University in New Jersey, respectively, as a Visiting Research Fellow.

Dr. Datoo left the academia in 1977 to enter the field of marketing research and consulting. He has worked for a couple of leading firms in New Jersey and Pennsylvania as a Senior Vice President focusing on the application of advanced statistical and modeling techniques to business marketing issues.